Welcome!

I'm a child of the first home-computing revolution. Back in the 1980s, I learned to program on a ZX Spectrum plugged into a portable colour TV, using a cassette deck for saving and loading games. Since the mid-1990s, much of my living has been earned by using the skills I began learning on that primitive, rubber-keyed chunk of plastic.

The Raspberry Pi brings the same opportunities to today's would-be programmers. A fully working computer the size of a credit card that you can buy for less than £30, the Pi is the ideal platform for learning about programming everything from games to robots.

Raspberry Pi for Beginners aims to help you get started as a coder by encouraging you to create your own programs. (Don't worry if you don't have a Raspberry Pi yet; our advice applies to Windows users too.) We cover just the theory you must know and then put those concepts to work in building two games – one simple and one more complex.

Why games? Because they're a great way to learn programming: they're fun, you get to play them, and they include all the ingredients common to most coding projects, from software utilities to robotic control. They can also lead to a great career as a games programmer.

But the real power of the Raspberry Pi is in its ability to connect with the real world – and this, along with its compact size, low cost and modest power requirements, makes it ideal for both mobile and remote purposes.

So in this book we also show you how to create an independent weather station that can be sited anywhere that has power and Wi-Fi. It's a great thing to do, and could open your mind to all sorts of possibilities. How about sending the Pi into space; using it as a CCTV controller; configuring it as the brains of a robot; or even using it to control home appliances?

So let's get started. Fasten your seat belt and welcome to the world of coders, tinkerers, makers and rocket scientists.

Kevin Partner

Contents

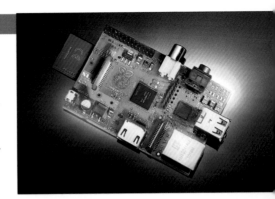

Chapter One
....

The Raspberry Pi story

Photography, Danny Bird; repro, Jan Cihak

Back in 2006, the Computer Laboratory at the University of Cambridge had a problem. Fewer and fewer students were applying to study computer science at the university, and the skill levels of those who did apply were declining year on year. Whereas, in the past, undergraduates had typically arrived at the university with some coding experience, by the mid-noughties most knew much more about PowerPoint than about programming.

This was partly due to a switch in emphasis at school towards teaching office applications and web design rather than how to program, but it was also because the earlier generation of home computers had been replaced by games consoles. Why did that matter? Because a ZX Spectrum, BBC Model B or Commodore 64 could be used **both** to play games **and** create software. The PlayStation 3 and Xbox, for all their technological superiority, are sealed units with no way for the average user to create their own games.

Perhaps the biggest problem, however, is caused by the way in which the internet has become part of everyday life. The average household now has at least one computer, usually a laptop, which they use for everything from banking through online shopping to social networking and playing games. The idea of handing over this now critical piece of kit to an inexperienced student of programming fills the rest of the family with fear – what if their experiments led to a problem with their internet banking or, worse, Facebook? What if their prospective programmer wanted to use it for hours at a time? What would they use for their Ocado shop?

There's another problem with modern laptops – they're simply over-the-top for learning to program on. Over-powered, distracting and complicated, today's operating systems are a million miles away from the blinking cursor of the classic home computer.

So, led by then-director of studies Eben Upton, the group that would one day become the Raspberry Pi Foundation set itself the target of encouraging 1,000 new computer science students across the UK. Since they couldn't directly re-write the syllabus taught in schools, they decided to focus on what they **could** do – so they began work on a new type of computer that would be easy to program and, critically, cheap to buy.

Fast-forward to February 2012 and, after a six-year journey, component suppliers Farnell and RS Electronics opened their websites for pre-orders of the Raspberry Pi. Though the project had been started with the aim of producing 1,000 units per year, initial interest was such that 10,000 were planned for production in 2012. Within minutes of going live with their Raspberry Pi order pages, both websites had collapsed and the initial allocation had disappeared in a wisp of smoke. A few days later, 100,000 pre-orders had been taken, with around a million units estimated to have shipped in 2012.

An education edition is due to be launched at a price that would allow a school to buy a dozen Raspberry Pis for the cost of one budget laptop – expect to see one in a school near you soon. The foundation has also launched an even cheaper version, called the Model A, with a lower specification. This guide focuses on the more capable Model B.

The perfect platform for learning programming

The Pi has been designed from the ground up to provide the ideal environment for learning programming – whether that's simply for the fun of it or as the start of a career in coding. It's cheap, compact and rugged, and it also comes with most of the tools you need to create your own programs built into its default software.

It may not be as fast as the family laptop, but think about this: the computer controlling the Mars Curiosity rover currently trundling across the surface of the red planet is less powerful than a £30 Raspberry Pi. If NASA's chip can power a space probe, just imagine what you can do with your Pi.

What is the Raspberry Pi?

The first thing you'll notice when you clap eyes on a Raspberry Pi is that it's tiny – the size of a credit card. Then you'll notice that it has no case – it's simply a printed circuit board. Despite its diminutive size and Heath Robinson appearance, however, the Pi is a completely functional computer. And it costs around £30. Let's take a look at what makes it tick.

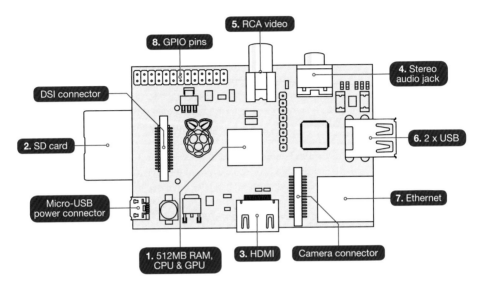

Brains
A single chip (**1**) contains memory, the central processing unit and graphics chip.

CPU (Central Processing Unit or Processor)
The Raspberry Pi uses a mobile phone chip designed by ARM – the company that designs the processors used in the majority of smartphones and tablets, including those sold by Apple. The version used in the Pi is slower than you'll find in an iPad, for example, but it's fast enough to do the job it's intended for.

GPU (Graphics Processing Unit)
Unlike the relatively pedestrian CPU, the Graphics Processing Unit on the Pi is equivalent to a top-of-the-line mobile device. It can run 3D games and play high-definition video (indeed, one of the most common uses for the Pi is as a very cheap media centre). With the right software, a TV and a broadband link you have iPlayer, YouTube and other internet video services at your fingertips.

Memory

The Pi comes with 512MB of Random Access Memory (RAM) – plenty for the uses we're going to put it to. It also comes with an SD card slot (**2**) – exactly the same as that used by many digital cameras – which takes the place of the hard disk found in most laptops. Programs are stored on the SD card and, once the Pi is powered on, these are copied into the much faster RAM until the computer is turned off, when the RAM is cleared. One great convenience of the Pi is that you can turn it from a media player to a desktop computer simply by swapping out the SD card – much easier than removing a laptop's hard disk!

Sound and vision

One of the design requirements for the Raspberry Pi was that it should be easy to hook up to existing equipment, so it includes an HDMI port (**3**) for connecting to a TV or computer monitor. HDMI carries both picture and sound, so if you use a monitor, you may need to plug a set of speakers into the stereo audio jack (**4**). If your monitor doesn't have an HDMI socket, you can buy a cheap adaptor to convert it to DVI – just bear in mind that you won't be able to use a monitor that has only a VGA connector.

If you're really stuck, you can use the RCA video jack (**5**) to connect to the composite video input on an old-fashioned CRT TV. However, this was added mainly to allow the Pi to be used in the Third World where TVs are more common than monitors – the picture quality is poor.

Connections

The Raspberry Pi comes with two USB ports (**6**) that you can use to connect a keyboard, mouse, Wi-Fi dongle or any compatible peripheral. You'll probably want to buy a USB hub to allow you to plug in multiple devices at once – just make sure it has a separate power adaptor; the Pi's ports supply only a low voltage.

You can connect the Raspberry Pi directly to your router or a wired network via the standard Ethernet port (**7**) – this gives the fastest and most reliable connection to the internet.

Pi Pins

So far, everything we've described (apart from the SD card) is pretty standard to all computers. However, the Pi has some extra capabilities not found on your common or garden laptop. The most important of these are the General Purpose Input Output (GPIO) pins (**8**), which offer various ways to control devices and receive input from sensors and such like. However, misusing these pins can bake your Pi so it's best to use one of the many add-on boards that allow you to experiment safely. We cover some of the options later.

The Pi also includes a connector for a camera module and a DSI connector for connecting the Pi to certain specialist displays such as mobile phone screens.

> **Focus On** The possibilities

So, this is a small, cheap computer with no moving parts and the ability to connect with the outside world. Put another way, imagine having the power of a laptop without its bulk or its fragility. With a Raspberry Pi you can take computing almost anywhere – think about the possibilities.

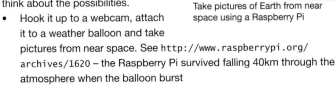

Take pictures of Earth from near space using a Raspberry Pi

- Hook it up to a webcam, attach it to a weather balloon and take pictures from near space. See `http://www.raspberrypi.org/archives/1620` – the Raspberry Pi survived falling 40km through the atmosphere when the balloon burst
- Attach temperature, humidity and air-pressure sensors to create an intelligent weather station
- Create a media centre for the car or home
- Build it into a bird box, along with infrared trip sensors and a webcam, to record the nesting season. See `http://www.youtube.com/watch?v=_-JpbFBCndo`
- Put together a very cheap internet radio
- Use it as the brains of a robot...as well as a general-purpose (if a little slow) computer. For less than £30!

And that's just the beginning.

Where can I get one?

The Raspberry Pi Foundation selected Premier Farnell (`http://uk.farnell.com/raspberry-pi`) and RS Electronics (`http://uk.rs-online.com/web/generalDisplay.html?id=raspberrypi`) to be its official suppliers, so we recommend buying direct from them. Whilst units are also available on eBay, Amazon and through some retailers,

RS Electronics is one of the two authorised suppliers of Raspberry Pi units in the UK

you're likely to get the lowest price and the latest models by going direct. As an example, in September 2012, when the foundation launched a slightly revised version of the Pi that included double the memory of the original model, customers of Farnell and RS Electronics automatically received the new version.

If you don't have an SD card already then you may want to add one to your order when you buy your Pi – that way you'll know it's compatible (although the vast majority of bog-standard cards work fine). Either way, a 4GB-8GB card is about the right size.

We **don't** recommend that you buy one with the operating system (OS) already installed. This is because the Raspberry Pi is designed to be a "hands on" computer and you'll learn a lot more about how things work by installing the OS yourself. Sooner rather than later you'll want to upgrade the OS, so it makes sense to familiarise yourself with the process right at the outset. It isn't difficult and you'll also save yourself a few pounds.

Setting up your Raspberry Pi

Once the jiffy bag containing your tiny new computer lands on the mat, you have a little work to do before you can connect it to a display and boot it up. The Raspberry Pi uses a standard SD card instead of the hard disk you'll find in most laptops, and your first job is to install the software needed to run the computer onto the SD card. It's not difficult, just follow the steps.

▶ Focus On ▶ Raspbian

There wouldn't be much point in a £30 computer if you were then required to install an expensive OS on it (such as Windows or Apple's OS X) to get it to work. This, and the fact that no version of Windows or OS X will work on the ARM chip of the Pi, means that the various OSes created for it are all based on the free and open-source Linux.

The foundation recommends Raspbian, a version of Debian that's a popular distribution of Linux. If this sounds like gobbledygook, don't worry – if you've used Windows, you'll find Raspbian pretty familiar.

You can even install Linux versions of many of the programs you're familiar with including LibreOffice for Microsoft-compatible word processing and spreadsheet work, and even the Chrome browser – we'll cover how to do this shortly. You'd be hard-pressed to find any computing activity for which mature, competent software doesn't exist for Raspbian.

Step 1: Prepare your SD card

1. You'll need a Windows-based computer for this. If your PC has an SD card slot, then go right ahead and insert your 4GB+ card. If not, you'll need to use an adaptor. **Red Alert:** If you use an external hard drive, then **disconnect it now** so there's no risk of accidentally picking the wrong drive letter when you reformat the SD card.

2. Next we need to write the Raspbian image to the SD card. We'll use a utility called "Image Writer for Windows" to do this. Go to `http://sourceforge.net/projects/win32diskimager/` and download the most recent version. Make sure you get the Binary (`win32diskimager-binary.zip`), not the source version.

3. Go to your Downloads folder, right-click on `win32diskimager-binary.zip` and select "Extract all". You'll then be asked to pick a folder into which to copy the files it contains.

4. Now, go to `http://www.raspberrypi.org/downloads` and find the Raspbian links – choose the one next to "Direct Download". Again, go to your Downloads folder, right-click and extract it – there will be only one file (it has the extension IMG)

5. Double-click `Win32DiskImage.exe`. Click the blue folder icon and use the "file open" box to find the IMG file you just extracted. Under Device, select your SD card from the list – **be very careful** to choose the correct drive letter for the SD card. Once you've checked this, click Write to transfer the image onto the card. That's it: your SD card is now ready to use.

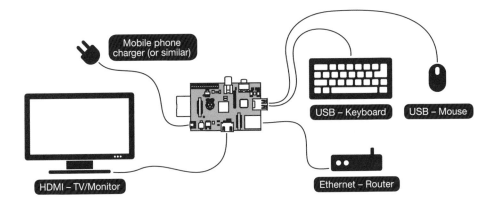

Stage 2: Hook up your Raspberry Pi

1. Connect the HDMI lead to your TV or monitor (hint: if your monitor doesn't have HDMI but does have DVI, you can buy a cheap adaptor). Now, connect the keyboard and mouse to the USB ports and the Ethernet port to your internet router or network. If you don't plan to use the Raspberry Pi near your router, you can use a compatible Wi-Fi dongle (a good example being the Edimax EW-7811UN)

The configuration screen may look dauntingly technical, but the options we want are easy to set

2. Now connect the power. Almost immediately, you'll see text streaming down the screen like a scene from *The Matrix*. When you first use an SD card, the Pi will boot to a configuration screen with various options – you can move up and down the list with the arrow keys, along with Enter and Escape. By default, the Raspberry Pi will use only 2GB of space: if your SD card is larger than this, select the **expand_rootfs** option and the entire capacity will become available. The **memory_split** option sets the proportion of memory that's assigned to the main CPU and how much to the video chip. For our purposes, we want the maximum for the CPU, so select this option.

   Now select **overclock** and set the value to "modest" – this speeds up the processor a little without drawing any more power. Finally, move down to the **boot_behaviour** option and set the Pi to boot into the Desktop view. Select <Finish> and the Pi will reboot.

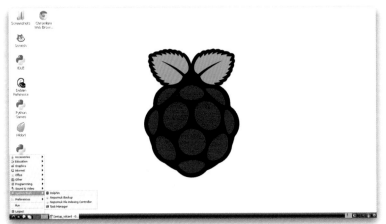

The Pi desktop is easy to get started with, especially if you're familiar with Windows

3. All being well, your Raspberry Pi will reboot into a desktop view that, on the surface at least, is pretty familiar. At the bottom-left you'll see the equivalent of Windows 7's Start button, for accessing the software that's pre-installed on the Raspberry Pi. Next to the Start button is an icon that launches the File Manager, which works in a similar way to the Windows File Explorer.

4. You'll also notice an icon labelled "LXTerminal", which, when double-clicked, launches a window containing the text pi@raspberrypi in green at the top left. We'll use this window to type various commands – don't worry, you'll only ever need to learn a few.

Stage 3: Find and install software

The Raspberry Pi comes with a basic range of software, but one of the benefits of a Linux-based system is a huge library of additional free programs.

Finding and installing software for the Raspberry Pi is very different to its Windows equivalent, however. Rather than running a setup program, with Linux you use a "package manager" and in many cases this is done by typing in commands. Don't panic, it's easy! We'll show you how via the terminal first because most online examples use this approach.

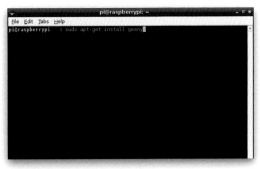

Installing software via the terminal isn't at all difficult once you know how

▶ **Focus On** ▶ **Wireless**

As a general rule, Linux distributions have poorer support for wireless networking than Windows PCs or Macs, since not all manufacturers write Linux drivers for their products. This also applies to wireless keyboards and mice, so you must make sure that a device is compatible with your Raspberry Pi before purchasing. You can find a list of supported devices at `http://elinux.org/RPi_VerifiedPeripherals`. The Edimax EW-7811UN Wi-Fi dongle is a good choice for most situations because, as well as being compatible, it performs well despite its diminutive size.

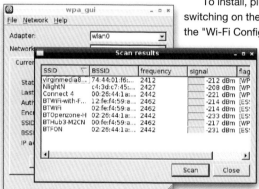

To install, plug it into the Raspberry Pi before switching on the PC. Once booted up, double-click the "Wi-Fi Config" icon on the desktop and choose the **Manage Networks** tab. Now click the **Add** button and you should see a list of nearby wireless networks. Select yours by double-clicking it and then complete the Network Properties dialog box – remembering to enter your wireless password into the PSK field. Now click **Add** and you should find you're connected.

Each distribution of Linux comes with a library of optional software, called Package Repositories. You can think of the initial setup as a starting point, to which you can then add software from the repositories to suit your purpose.

For a general-purpose computer, you'd probably want to install an office suite such as LibreOffice (a version of OpenOffice), and the Chromium browser (the open-source version of Google Chrome). In this case, we're going to install Chromium and then focus mainly on installing a programming editor. At various points throughout the book, we'll add extra packages.

1. Let's begin by installing Chromium. Double-click LXTerminal and type:

```
sudo apt-get update
```

...followed by the Enter key. This probably looks incomprehensible, so let's take it step by step. The first command, `sudo`, tells Linux that you want to run the rest of the commands as a "super-user". This is similar to the Administrator user in Windows – it gives permission to change the system.

This can be dangerous if not used properly, so, we have to explicitly type sudo to confirm we want to do so. apt is short for "Advanced Packaging Tool" and this is the program that installs our software. get is the utility within apt that does this – it **gets** packages.

Finally "update" tells apt-get to download the latest list of packages: you should always update apt-get before trying to install software.

2. Now, to actually install Chromium we can type:

```
sudo apt-get install chromium
```

...and Enter. This time we tell apt-get to "install" a named package. Your terminal window will now fill up with lines of text explaining what it's doing as the software automatically installs. When it's done, Chromium will be available from the Internet submenu of the Start button. To place an icon on the desktop, right-click the icon in the submenu and select "Add to desktop".

3. This is all very well, but how do you know what to install and what the package name is? One way is to Google "office software for Raspberry Pi", but another is to install a graphical package manager. Type:

```
sudo apt-get install synaptic
```

This will download and install the Synaptic Package Manager. Once this is done, you will find it by clicking the Start button and choosing the Other submenu. Click Synaptic and you'll be asked to type your password (which, unless you've changed it, will be "raspberry"). You'll now see a window containing all the packages available to the Raspberry Pi, organised by type.

4. We're going to use Synaptic to install a code editor called Geany. On the left side of the Synaptic window, scroll down to the Development category. Now scroll through the right-hand window until you find Geany. In fact, you need to click the package **geany-common** first, then select Mark for Installation, before doing the same with the **geany** package. Once you've done this, click the Apply button to install it. This is straightforward, but remember the equivalent command in the terminal would be:

```
sudo apt-get install geany
```

...which is clearly much quicker. So, if you know the package name, you should use the command line approach; if you want to browse, choose Synaptic. Why not give it a go and install LibreOffice?

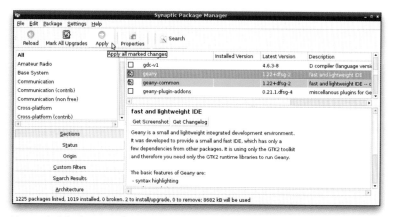

You can install whatever software takes your fancy – and it's all free!

The flip side

You now have a fully working Pi, ready and raring to go. But while you think about all the possibilities opening up before you, bear in mind the following.

The Pi is slow. If you're used to the snappiness of a modern computer, using heavyweight software such as LibreOffice will feel like wading through treacle. You'll notice a delay of a couple of seconds after you double-click an icon before anything seems to happen, for example. This is partly because an SD card isn't as fast as a modern hard disk when it comes to reading files, as well as reflecting the speed of the processor. Once your word processor has fully loaded, you'll probably find the performance perfectly acceptable. Some games will work well on the Pi too – 3D shoot-em-up Quake was famously ported across very early on. However, the Pi is not designed for playing high-end games, so don't imagine it will replace an Xbox for that purpose.

Linux is not Windows/OS X. Although the Raspberry Pi desktop looks superficially similar to Windows, underneath the surface there are many differences. You can achieve in Raspbian just about anything you could accomplish in Windows or OS X – but allow yourself extra time for research.

Not all hardware will work. Partly because the Pi runs a variety of Linux and partly because it uses an ARM chip, some keyboards, mice, printers, Wi-Fi dongles and other peripherals won't work. You should always check the list of approved hardware or, if buying online, check the reviews to see if others state the product works with the Raspberry Pi.

Having said all that, most people will consider these limitations a small price to pay for a tiny, portable, durable computer costing around £30 that can open up a huge range of creative possibilities.

Photography, Danny Bird; repro, Jan Cihak

Chapter Two

What is programming?

Mention the word "programming" to most people and one of two images will pop into their minds – the T-shirted hacker wreaking havoc with sensitive government servers, or lines of incomprehensible code streaming down a screen. Not surprisingly, real programming is nothing like either.

Wikipedia defines programming as "the process of designing, writing, testing, debugging, and maintaining the source code of computer programs", which is a bit like saying that running is something you do when you run. Of course, programming means to write code – but what does that code do? What is the point of creating it?

The fact is that every single electronic device you might come across in your daily life is controlled by code that was written by a programmer. It's barely an exaggeration to say that programming is what makes the modern world go round. By learning how to code, then, you are equipping yourself with the knowledge and skills you need to take an active part in shaping the environment you and others live in.

Whilst that might sound a little grand or abstract, just remember that a person, or a team of people, created the code that runs the microwave you use to make cheesy beans for supper, the fuel injection system that gets you from A to B, and the set-top box you use to watch your time-shifted TV programmes – as well as the more obvious code you encounter on your computer, games console or smartphone.

Someone must write the instructions that make these devices carry out their useful functions and, despite what you might imagine, you don't need to be a genius to code. Above all else, programming involves two main skills: creative imagination and the ability to think in a logical, structured way. It certainly doesn't involve remembering every obscure command of every coding language (that's Google's job). Programming is a process in the same sense as planning a presentation, cooking a complex meal or coming up with next season's Fantasy Football strategy. It's like solving a puzzle and it's one of the most enjoyable and creative things you'll ever do.

Don't believe me? Just have a little patience and you'll soon discover the thrill of taking control of your computer rather than feeling a slave to it. This is at the heart of programming: having an impact in the real world whether that's on a PC screen, smartphone or a hacked-together robot trundling after the dog. This impact can be profound and, when the penny drops, you'll realise that programming frees you from being a passenger in this technological world and provides the toolkit to take hold of the wheel for yourself.

Setting your sights

With such a wealth of possibilities it's important to think about what *you* want to achieve with your programming skills. Having a practical goal in mind will help make sense of what you're learning, as well as providing an opportunity to practise and get a sense of real achievement. The best advice is to follow your

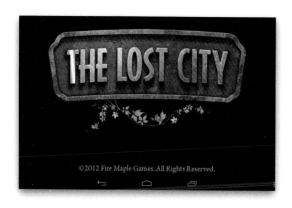

interests and choose a project you'll enjoy. Whether or not you want to become a professional programmer, by focusing on something that you'll enjoy for its own sake, you'll become better quicker. The people at the top of the industry, earning the significant pay cheques by creating the software

The Lost City is a premium game for smartphones and tablets created by indie programmer Joe Kauffman. It has been installed around 500,000 times on Android devices alone

that runs the banks and major businesses, for example, almost always began this way – and many continue to code for fun in their spare time.

So what is achievable for a keen beginner willing to invest some time, effort and brainpower to learn programming skills?

Making games

Most coders begin by creating games because most like playing games. Whether you realise it or not, when you play a game you're gaining an understanding of how games work. Crucially, this means you know what you're aiming for when developing your own game.

The games category covers everything from basic word-guessing puzzles through 2D platform adventures to immersive first-person extravaganzas such as the Call of Duty series. As a new programmer, you'll begin at the simple end before settling on your favourite form; many people choose arcade puzzlers or point-and-click adventures, for example, because these can be created in small teams or even by coders working alone. Whatever your ultimate ambition, games are a great way to learn programming.

Mobile apps

The market for smartphone and tablet apps has become hugely popular in the past few years, especially amongst "indie" developers (that's you). One reason for this is that mobile devices represent the fastest growing category of internet-connected hardware. Even more importantly, each main platform (iOS, Android, BlackBerry and Windows) is served by marketplaces that make it easy for individual developers to publish their work. You don't need to sign a deal with a major distributor such as EA Games to get your masterpiece into the hands of your audience: you can create it and publish it direct, at minimal cost.

That's not to say it's all plain-sailing. Despite what you might hear, mobile app development is no gravy train. But it is the leading modern platform and a good sector to learn in if you're looking for a career in programming.

Web development

By creating applications that run on a web server, you potentially gain all the benefits of developing apps for mobile devices as well as having your software available to the billions of users of standard PCs. Whilst there are many situations where a native app is a better choice (games being one), it's often most effective to put the code on the web and have people access it via a browser.

Much of this programming goes unnoticed, but it's there lurking in the background every time you order something from Amazon or post a status update on Facebook. Anything that happens on the web beyond serving up static web pages is programming. To see an example of just how stunning this can be, take a look at http://www.movikantirevo.com.

Core Temp is a utility program that lives up to its name: it monitors the internal temperature of a PC's components

PC applications

There's still a big market for software that users download and run on their computers. This can include utilities, games, educational software and creative programs such as music editors and art packages. In practice, this usually means that you spot a problem that needs solving and, if you can't find a good pre-existing solution to it, you write your own program. You'd be amazed at the tiny niches some of this software serves – there are, for example, several "explosion generator" applications that satisfy the need for arcade game developers to blow up enemy spaceships in spectacular style.

Typically, the coder hacks together a solution to their own problem and then, if they think there would be an audience for it, spends time adding an effective user interface (windows, dialogue boxes and buttons) before releasing it for general use. It's also common to contribute the code to the open-source community, which means that anyone can amend and update it. Done in an organised way, this can result in a much better, more widely used program – for which you receive the main credit. Very good for your CV!

Controlling your home

With the Raspberry Pi and related technologies such as the Arduino (www. arduino.cc), it's become much simpler to program real-world objects as well as traditional computers. There's nothing quite as cool as connecting with your environment, whether that's keeping tabs on your energy bills, watching a robot you've made from an old remote control toy make its way around the living room floor, or taking pictures from a weather balloon. The range of possibilities is infinite and it's in this area that the Raspberry Pi has a big advantage over a laptop, say – its diminutive size, modest power requirements, robustness and, above all, low cost make it ideal for real-world projects.

And that's only the beginning. As you develop your programming skills, you'll notice more opportunities to put them to work. So, enough explanation: now it's time to tool up and get cracking.

What do you need?

If you want to be a coder, you'll need both hardware and software to get started. The good news is that the hardware is cheap – and the software is free. By using a version of Linux as the operating system, you can learn to code on a low-cost computer such as the Raspberry Pi or a repurposed laptop or desktop that's now too slow to run Windows. Popular Linux variants such as Raspbian, Debian and Ubuntu are free, as is most of the software you can run on them – including many of the most popular programming languages.

Parlez-vous Python?

The first decision you need to make is which programming language to learn. There are hundreds to choose from, but a good choice would be one that's widely used, easy to learn, applicable to lots of programming tasks, and similar enough to other languages to make it easy to spread your wings later. It should also be free to download and use. At bit.ly/ tiobe_index you'll find a table of languages in order of their popularity, in terms of jobs and online resources. The only candidate that meets all our criteria is Python. Here's why:

- **It's widely used.** Python appears in the top ten of the TIOBE index (at the time of writing), which means that many skilled engineers use it and there are many jobs for Python programmers. Plus, there are plenty of resources to help learn it, including this book.

- **It's easy to learn.** The Raspberry Pi Foundation chose Python as its recommended programming language for this reason. One way to describe a language is to say how "high level" it is: broadly speaking, the more English-like it looks, the more high level it's considered. Take a look at the following code. It shows how to simply make the words "Hello World!" appear on-screen, and it's written in C, a very widely used but low-level language:

```
#include <stdio.h>
int main(int argc, char *argv[])
{
    printf("Hello world!\n");
    return 0;
}
```

Don't worry if you didn't follow that – it's clear that there's a considerable learning curve involved in understanding C, let alone creating it for yourself. Now, for comparison, let's look at another section of code that does exactly the same thing, only this time written in Python:

```
print ("Hello World!")
```

Not only is this Python example much closer to English, and therefore easier to understand, it's also much shorter – in this case reducing six lines of low-level C into a single concise instruction. This is another characteristic feature of high-level languages.

- **It's flexible.** You've probably heard of BASIC, which is another well-known and easy-to-learn language. However, these days BASIC isn't as popular as it used to be. Visual Basic is the only dialect that appears in the top ten and it's restricted to Windows computers; the commercial version is also relatively expensive. Python, on the other hand, can be used on Windows, Mac and Linux computers, as well as on many other platforms. It's also able to access libraries of code created in C and C++.

- **It's a good first language.** The concepts that underpin Python are similar to those found in other popular languages. So once you've learned to code in Python, you'll find it much easier to get to grips with almost any other mainstream language.

And if you need any other reason… it's named after Monty Python!

▶ **Focus On ▶ Python squared**

There are two families of Python in common use: 2.x and 3.x. This probably seems odd, as it's usually the case that when a new version of any software is released (Python 3 was released in 2008) users tend to upgrade. However, one of Python's great strengths is the huge library of add-ons created by the Python community and some of these are written in version 2, making them incompatible with the latest version.

The differences between versions 2 and 3 aren't huge so, in this book, we're focusing on Python 2.7 – the version that comes installed by default in Raspbian at the time of writing this book. This means we can use just about every available Python library but still move interchangeably between it and version 3 when the time comes.

Tools of the trade

Even though you already own a Raspberry Pi, it's often more convenient to develop on another, more powerful computer and then move the code across to the Pi. Even if you've set up the Pi in your living room, hidden it in a shed or built it into a toy robot, this can be a convenient way to work, since it's very easy to connect to the Pi across a network.

The good news is that an old laptop – or a modern PC or Mac – will do fine for Pi development. However, whilst Python is available for all the main operating systems, its natural home is Linux. If you're using Windows or OS X, it's a good idea to install a Linux distribution alongside your existing operating system – or, even better, set up a dedicated computer.

Wubi allows you to install the Ubuntu flavour of Linux alongside Windows, but we recommend installing it on a dedicated computer

Ubuntu

If you're using a Raspberry Pi, you should already be set up with Raspbian. What if you want to stick with your existing PC? You can install Python for Windows, but we recommend using Linux as the basis of your programming environment. Why? Well, it's Python's natural environment and if you intend to do any serious coding you'll almost certainly encounter Linux at some point, especially if you develop for the internet.

On top of this, Linux is *made* for tinkering; it's a much more open OS than either Windows or OS X, and has an active community providing all the bits and pieces you need to create great programs. You can also find plenty of generous and enthusiastic advice.

For most people, Ubuntu is the best Linux distribution to choose. It's based on Debian (like Raspbian) but is more user friendly. It's the most widely used and most actively developed version of Linux. You can also install it in several ways, depending on your situation.

1. **Wipeout.** If you want to repurpose an old laptop then your best bet is probably to wipe whatever version of Windows is already on it and replace it with Ubuntu (having backed up any documents you want to keep). To do this, go to www.ubuntu.com/download/desktop and download the newest 32-bit version. The download is in the form of an ISO file, which you can either burn to DVD (double-click it and follow the prompts) or transfer to a USB flash drive. When you're ready to install it on the target computer, insert the DVD or flash drive and follow the prompts. Full instructions are on the Ubuntu downloads page.

2. **Sibling rivalry.** Another option is to install Ubuntu alongside Windows so you can use both. To do this, download the WUBI Windows installer from www.ubuntu.com/download/desktop/windows-installer. This is a standard Windows program that downloads and runs the Ubuntu setup. As part of the process, your hard disk is divided up into sections so that Ubuntu and Windows can co-exist; make sure you have backed up your PC before starting. Once Ubuntu is successfully installed, you'll choose which OS to use when you boot up your computer. It's also easy to uninstall Ubuntu from within Windows.

3. **Virtually Ubuntu.** Perhaps the most flexible option is to set up Ubuntu as a "virtual machine" (VM) running in Windows. A VM is a software program that pretends it's a hardware computer running your chosen operating system (in this case, Ubuntu). The great benefit of this approach is that if something were to go wrong, you could very quickly wipe it and start again. To create a VM, you need software such as Oracle's VirtualBox (www.virtualbox.org/wiki/Downloads). Once your virtualisation software is installed, you can set up a VM and then load the Ubuntu ISO file into it. In fact, you can create as many VMs for which you have space, allowing you to try out any number of different versions of Linux.

Of the three approaches, using WUBI to install alongside Windows is the simplest, whereas the VM option is the most flexible but requires more technical confidence.

▶ **Focus On ▶ Python on Windows**

Windows is the only major operating system that doesn't come with Python built in. If, for whatever reason, you're forced to work in Windows, you should download the Windows installer at www.python.org/getit. Choose the latest version of Python 2.7. Don't choose a 64-bit version (you'll see the number "64" in the description) since this would make it incompatible with many important libraries.

- Python 2.7.3 Windows Installer (Windows binary -- does not include source)
- Python 2.7.3 Windows X86-64 Installer (Windows AMD64 / Intel 64 / X86-64 binary [1] -- does not include source)
- Python 2.7.3 Mac OS X 64-bit/32-bit x86-64/i386 Installer (for Mac OS X 10.6 and later [2])
- Python 2.7.3 Mac OS X 32-bit i386/PPC Installer (for Mac OS X 10.3 through 10.6 [2])
- Python 2.7.3 compressed source tarball (for Linux, Unix or Mac OS X)
- Python 2.7.3 bzipped source tarball (for Linux, Unix or Mac OS X, more compressed)

To set up Python on Windows, choose the latest installer (2.7.3 at the time of writing). **Don't** choose the 64-bit version, shown on the second line

The programmer's toolkit

There are three things you'll need for most coding tasks: a programming language, an editor, and – if your project is going to make use of graphics and sound – a set of software tools for creating and editing these resources.

Programming language

The Raspberry Pi comes with Python 2.7 built in. This is the final version of the Python 2 family and the code examples in this book are aimed at version 2.7. When the educational version of the Raspberry Pi is released, it's possible that it will default to Python 3, but it will almost certainly also include version 2.7 – and this is the one we recommend you use. We'll cover how to make sure you're targeting the right version below.

Editor

Computer programs are usually text files, which means you can edit them using any word processor or text editor. However, by using an IDE (Integrated Development Environment) rather than, for example, Leafpad (the Raspberry Pi's equivalent of Windows Notepad), you get access to all sorts of tools that help with your programming.

Raspbian includes two versions of an editor called IDLE – one for Python 2.7 and one for Python 3 – but it's rather too basic for convenient programming. For that reason, we've created the examples in this book using a more advanced editor called Geany. If you followed the walkthrough in part 1 to set up your Raspberry Pi, then you've probably already installed Geany. If not, simply open up LXTerminal and type:

```
sudo apt-get update
sudo apt-get install geany
```

...and press Enter. The first line ensures the list of packages on your Raspberry Pi is up to date, the second line performs the actual install. If you're using Windows, go to www.geany.org/Download/Releases and select the latest version of the Full Installer.

Media

Many projects require custom graphics, and for games you'll probably need to create or edit your own sound effects. As with text editors, there are many choices available to Linux users but the gloriously named "GNU Image Manipulation Program", or GIMP to its adherents, is the most fully featured and best supported. For sound editing, the best choice is Audacity. Over the page, we'll describe how to find and install them both.

▶ Focus On ⟩ Geany

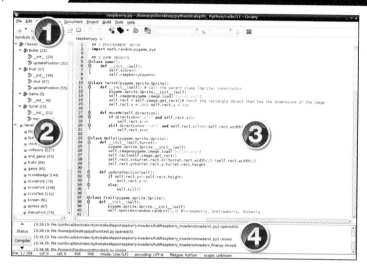

1. Toolbar

The Geany toolbar contains shortcuts for moving quickly through your code, picking and inserting colours and letting you test-run your program with a single click.

2. Code Explorer

The left-hand pane displays information about the program you're currently working on, including easy access to its main parts.

3. Coding Window

This is where you'll be spending most of your time. Geany includes:

- Code suggestion – the editor guesses what you're typing and offers to finish for you;
- In-built reference – when you type the name of a Python statement, it shows what that function expects to follow it and how it works;
- Syntax colouring – "syntax" refers to the words and numbers that make up your code, and by automatically applying different colours to different types of syntax, Geany makes code easy to read and debug.

4. Message Window

Geany displays messages and status reports in this window. You can also select the Terminal tab to get quick access to the LXTerminal.

GIMP

To install GIMP on your Raspberry Pi, start up Synaptic Package Manager and find gimp in the Graphics category. Select this and also gimp-data then click Apply. Alternatively, from LXTerminal, enter the following line:

```
sudo apt-get update
sudo apt-get install gimp
```

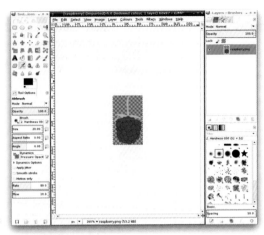

Once installed, you'll find an icon to run GIMP in the Graphics folder of your Start menu. Since GIMP is a processor-intensive application, it will run fairly slowly on your Raspberry Pi, but it's perfectly usable. To get the best performance, shut down any other applications before running it. Windows users can download the installer from http://gimp-win.sourceforge.net/stable.html. Whichever OS you're using, you'll find GIMP reasonably familiar if you've used any other photo-editing package, whether that's Windows Paint or Photoshop. You can find out more about GIMP at www.gimp.org.

GIMP contains all the image editing and creation tools you're likely to need

Audacity

Most games include sound effects and, even if you use pre-existing resources, the chances are you'll need to edit them to fit your project sooner or later. Audacity is a basic sound-editing package that includes all the features most people require – for free. In Synaptic, you'll find Audacity in the Multimedia category; again, you need to make sure that both audacity and audacity-data are selected before you click Apply. To install via LXTerminal:

```
sudo apt-get update
sudo apt-get install audacity
```

Bear in mind that if you've only just installed GIMP, you don't need to run the update command again.

Once installed, you'll find Audacity in the Sound & Video section of your Start menu. You can find more information and download links for Windows and Mac at http://audacity.sourceforge.net.

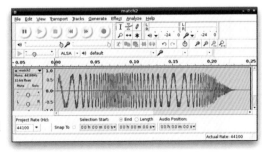

Audacity is an easy-to-use but capable sound editor

Let's get cracking

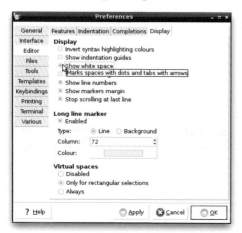

If everything is going to plan, our test program should display a working clock on the screen

The final step before we get into coding is to check that your Python environment is working as expected. Rather than bashing out the bog-standard "hello world" program, we're going to create a real-time clock for your desktop. This is not only more interesting and useful, it will also test whether you have two of the most important Python libraries installed and working, as well as Python itself.

1. Connect your Pi and load up the desktop. Open Geany by going to the Programming folder of the Start menu.

2. Click File, New and then immediately save it as "clock.py". The "py" extension tells Geany you're creating a Python file and switches on its built-in help and syntax colouring. Now, go to the Edit menu in Geany and click Preferences. Pick the Editor tab on the left followed by the Display tab along the top, then click next to "Show white space" to fill in the checkbox. This means that all spaces and tabs are marked in the editor window, which is helpful when typing and editing Python code.

3. Type the code from the listing below into Geany:

```
import time,pygame
pygame.init()
theFont=pygame.font.Font(None,72)
clock = pygame.time.Clock()
screen = pygame.display.set_mode([320, 200])
pygame.display.set_caption('Pi Time')
while True:
    clock.tick(1)
    theTime=time.strftime("%H:%M:%S",time.localtime())
    timeText=theFont.render(str(theTime), True,(255,255,255),(0,0,0))
    screen.blit(timeText,(80,60))
    pygame.display.update()
```

Be very careful to copy the code exactly, including every punctuation mark, and make sure you put line breaks in the correct places. Be particularly careful to use the tab key at the start of lines where needed, to indent your code exactly as it's shown in the listing. If you prefer, you can download the file from www.rpilab.net/code.

Although what you've just typed in probably looks like gobbledygook at the moment, you can see immediately how little code is needed to create a real, working application. For now, we're just testing that your setup is working so, once you've typed everything in and checked it for errors, click the Cog icon on the Geany toolbar to run the app. All being well, after a short pause, your clock will pop up and start ticking away. If so, congratulations: you've demonstrated that Geany, Python and the Pygame module are working together.

If the clock doesn't appear, don't despair – it's common for programs not to work first time. Take a look at the LXTerminal window, because it will contain a message that can help you diagnose the problem. More often than not, the cause will be a mistake you've made in typing the code, but another possible problem could be Python complaining that it's missing the Pygame module. If it is, and you're using a Raspberry Pi, the chances are that your machine has been set to run Python 3 by default. This is an easy problem to fix: go to the Build menu in Geany and select "Set Build Commands". In the field next to "Execute", remove the number 3 to set it to run the older version of Python.

4. Once the clock is working, you know Python is correctly installed and working on your Raspberry Pi. Congratulations: you now have everything you need to begin your career as a programmer. Let's go.

Programming – from the inside out

Computers, microcontrollers and other electronic devices are used for such a wide range of tasks that you might imagine they share very little in common. However, whether they're running on an Xbox, inside the dashboard of a car or controlling the Curiosity Mars Rover on the surface of the planet, most programs work in a fundamentally similar way: they take **input**, apply some sort of **logic** to it and then **output** the results.

Some very simple programs do this once each time they're run – for example, a calculator – but most applications go through this loop many times per second. As a programmer, then, almost every process you'll ever have to work with will fall into one of these three categories – and knowing how they work makes understanding how code is put together much simpler. Let's look at a few examples to see how this works in practice.

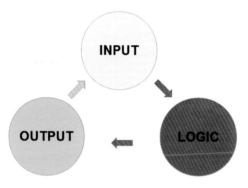

Any program can be broken down into its key elements – and doing so makes things much easier to understand

A VAT calculator (yawn!)

Yes, it's boring but somebody has to write programs to carry out useful, mundane tasks such as this. A VAT calculator would ask the user to type in an amount; it would then work out the VAT on that amount and add that to the original value to arrive at a total. Finally, the program would display the result on-screen.

In this case, then, the amount entered by the user is the input, the VAT calculation is the logic, and displaying the result on-screen is the output. Bear in mind that the output could just as easily be to a printer or even a speech synthesiser; however, if that was the case, neither of the first two parts would be affected. Whilst this might make little difference on a tiny app such as this, but on large corporate systems splitting the code into these three purposes makes it possible for different programmers to work on each and for the application to be easily ported from desktop to web to mobile.

Forza Motorsport for Xbox

This is more like it! In a driving game, the player uses a controller or steering wheel as input and the console then translates the directional changes and applies them to its calculations of the car's position using its logic code. Once it has done this, it generates and displays the output in the form of graphics on the screen. Given the frame rate of a modern console game, this is happening many times per second – not just for the visuals, but for the sound effects too. In that case, the input might be the controller buttons assigned to acceleration and braking, the logic involves applying the correct physics to the Xbox's model of the game world, and the output – along with the visual elements – includes the sound of a thrashed engine or screaming brakes.

Mars Rover

Right now, around 225 million miles away, a robot the size of a Ford Fiesta is wending its way across the surface of Mars. Controlling the Curiosity Mars Rover is a computer less powerful than a Raspberry Pi. This computer, the RAD750, created by a subsidiary of British company BAE Systems, contains over 2 million lines of code written in C (although Python was used to create testing scripts).

This code controls everything from sensing the environment to navigating the Rover through the Martian landscape. Since radio waves take more than 12 minutes to travel between Mission Control and Mars, the Rover can't be driven like a remote-control car. So it includes software that uses its cameras (input) to determine where rocks and other obstructions are, calculates a safe path (logic) and turns the wheels (output). Bear in mind that human beings wrote the code, and they started programming with as little knowledge as you may have right now.

Clock

Finally, remember the tiny clock app we created in the last section? It took the current system clock time as input, converted it to a human-readable form (logic) and displayed it on-screen (output).

Under the microscope

So most programs take input, process that information using logic and then output it in some form; we can use this information when we design and write our applications. For example, let's say you've decided to create an old-school arcade game. In your mind's eye you see different fruit falling from the top of the screen, some of them raspberries. The player uses a laser-gun that moves across the bottom of the screen attempting to shoot the raspberries but miss all the other fruit. Without some sort of model in mind, you'd struggle to work out where to begin and how to organise your thoughts. The ILO model gives you a template to help get started.

Input

Let's begin by thinking about what inputs the game will take from the user. During the game, the player needs a way of controlling the laser gun, so we need to decide if that's going to be achieved via keyboard, mouse or touch. The choice depends largely on the platform we're aiming at. In the case of the Raspberry Pi, keyboard is best, so we're going to track the left and right arrow keys, along with the spacebar for firing laser bolts. Why space? Because it's the convention. How do you know? By playing games. If you ever needed an excuse for trying out as many games as possible you can now do it in the name of research! Other inputs will include buttons for starting, choosing levels, exiting and help.

Output

Think about how the user will experience the game. First they'll see the fruit, laser and bullets appear on-screen and then move. So we'll need to write code for displaying these graphical elements and animating them. The player also needs to see a score and any other status information – perhaps a time limit and basic instructions – so we'll need a way to display information in text format. And then we'll need to write code to play the obligatory bleeps of the classic arcade game.

But output isn't just what the player sees or hears. If we want to store the players' high scores, we need to save the data somewhere. This is output even though it isn't visible to the user.

Logic

Whilst the player might notice the quality of graphics and animations, or how well the laser gun responds to their keyboard presses, far more effort will go into the behind-the-scenes tasks our program must carry out to make sure the game works as intended. Logic is the glue that links input to output: without it you might have falling fruit and rising bullets but no way of connecting the two.

In most cases, you'll find yourself spending the majority of your time writing logic code. For example, we must constantly send new co-ordinates for all the objects on the screen to the output code so it can accurately reflect their positions. We must check for collisions, and when one is detected we must react accordingly by updating the output and scores – as well as checking whether the game has finished. By breaking all these jobs down into smaller and smaller steps, you eventually end up at the level of the single programming task.

Mirror mirror

Most programs interact with a user in some way. In a game, it's the user that's providing the input in the first place. In fact, the player and the program become part of a cycle: the user sees the fruit descending (input), decides where to move the laser gun (logic), and presses the keys accordingly (output). Put another way, the output of your computer program becomes the player's input, and vice versa.

If you're designing a program that interacts with a user in this way, you must take account of the whole system. It's not enough to think about the best way for the code to accept input; you must also consider how the player can best provide it. For example, when choosing the best keys for moving the gun left and right, it may be more convenient from a programming point of view to choose A and B – but it makes much more sense for the user to use the left and right arrow keys. We've all used apps that have clearly been designed for the convenience of the programmer – remember that frustration when you come to create your own.

Modularise

So you've split the tasks your program needs to perform into input, logic and output: how does this translate into the real world of creating your game? It does this by helping you to work out how to organise your code. Imagine slicing a pie into equal parts. You could begin by cutting it into thirds, and then continuing to halve until you reach the optimum size. Input, logic and output are these thirds, which you then divide up into smaller units of programming. In Python these units are called Modules, Functions and Objects.

Modules

To create a Python program, you type code into an editor and save it. The saved file is a module so, in a way, every Python program could be called a module, even our tiny clock. However, typing all your code into a single file is rarely a good idea unless the app is very simple. More typically, you create a main script file, then split the rest of the code into separate files, each of which is a module.

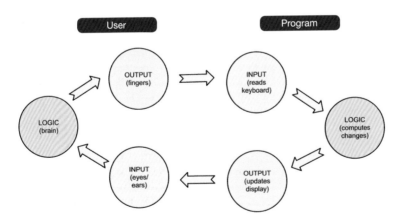

It's important to think in terms of how your code serves the user's needs and desires

For example, you might create a module for handling the display, one for saving the score and reading it back, and another to listen for the user's key presses. You would then make the code in those modules available to the main script by "importing" them. Take a look again at the first line of the clock code:

```
import time,pygame
```

As you've probably guessed, time and pygame are modules. time is built into all Python installations and is, in effect, part of the standard language, whereas pygame is a specialised module that helps in the development of games. Importing your own modules is done in exactly the same way.

Functions

Modules divide into functions: blocks of code that perform a specific task and have their own unique name. For example, in the "display" module for our game, we might have a function for drawing a bullet, another for painting the animated background, and a third for exploding the fruit. Within these functions you'll find our actual lines of code – so functions are the smallest subdivision.

Objects

Python is an object-oriented programming (OOP) language. This means the code that controls how parts of a program works is contained within those parts – as opposed to the procedural approach used by languages such as BASIC, which keep everything in a big central file. OOP makes it easier to build and maintain code, and it means we can effortlessly create multiple copies of objects.

For example, think about a game of Space Invaders. The invaders themselves are identical to each other and move left, right and down the screen. The procedural approach would be to draw each invader separately, one at a time, and keep track in memory of which one is where, whether it's been destroyed or has reached the bottom of the screen.

The object-oriented approach is to write code for one invader (this is called a Class) so that it keeps track of its own position and status, and then to create as many copies (called Instances) of that class as necessary. Once they're up and running, they each run independently.

As a rule, OOP means less code overall; programming that is much easier to understand (as you know that any code within the Invader class relates to the aliens); and, because of this simplicity, fewer bugs and better performance.

So, a Python program is usually made up of modules containing functions and classes (which also contain functions). Despite their somewhat intimidating names, modules, functions and classes are simply ways of organising code, and they're there to make life easier. With that behind us, it's time to dive into Python.

Photography: Danny Bird; repro, Jan Cihak

Chapter Three

Programming in Python

So, you've set up the Raspberry Pi and you've got a basic grasp of the principles of programming under your belt. It's time to start learning the practical skills needed to create Python programmes.

In this section of the book you'll find many code samples. These are all short and I strongly recommend you type them in: doing so will help you gain familiarity with the structure of a Python program, and give you practice in using an editor and running programs. You can also download the full code from the book's companion website: www.rpilab.net.

Don't worry if you struggle with some of the concepts introduced in this section; we're going to cover a lot of ground quickly so we can move onto programming larger, more rewarding projects as quickly as possible. Whether you're aware of it or not, if you follow the examples, most of what you need to know will sink in and you'll then have plenty of opportunity to see how the fundamentals of Python work in action as we build the code for our projects in the following sections of the book.

Introducing Python

All programming languages have the same broad purpose: to provide a way for humans to control devices powered by a microprocessor. With most languages, code made up of letters, numbers and symbols is typed into an editor line by line before being run by the computer.

Python is a high-level language because the code itself is relatively English-like. Indeed, any competent programmer looking at a well-designed Python application should be able to work out what it is trying to achieve, whether or not they have ever learned the language itself. This makes Python a good first language and an excellent choice for a wide range of purposes. But how does it compare with English, for example?

English	Python	
Books	Programs	Books and programs tend to be about one thing – whether that's a story or a game.
Chapters	Modules	Books are split into chapters and programs into modules – the difference is that chapters are designed to be read in order whereas modules can be used multiple times.
Pages	Functions	Chapters are subdivided into pages but, again, they are presented in a linear order. Modules are made up of functions, each responsible for a specific task.
Paragraphs	Blocks	Usually blocks of code, within functions, are processed in the order they appear, just like paragraphs on a page.
Lines	Lines	Each line of a book contains one thought or idea – each line of a program contains one complete action.
Words, numbers and punctuation etc	Statements, commands, operators and separators etc	The nuts and bolts of both human and computer languages. To become a French speaker, you must learn French words, and how they are put together using grammar. To write Python code, you learn the various statements that have meaning in the language, and how they are put together in meaningful ways.

So, both human and machine languages have much in common. Perhaps the biggest difference is that while you don't have to speak perfect German to make yourself understood to a native, computers are entirely unforgiving: if you don't get your language 100% correct, they won't understand what you mean. This is because, at their digital hearts, computers understand only two conditions – 1 and 0, right and wrong – so there can be none of the ambiguity or guesswork of human communication. Fortunately, Python is much easier to learn than French, for example; when you get it wrong, only you and your Raspberry Pi will know. And the Pi won't tell.

```
1   import pygame,random
2   pygame.init()
3   clock = pygame.time.Clock()  # Clock to limit speed
4   WIDTH=600; HEIGHT=600; BLACK=(0,0,0)
5   screen = pygame.display.set_mode([WIDTH, HEIGHT])
6   screen.fill(BLACK)
7
8   def draw_circle(colour):
9       x=random.randint(1,WIDTH)
10      y=random.randint(1,HEIGHT)
11      size=random.randint(1,5)
12      pygame.draw.circle(screen,colour,(x,y),size)
13
14  def random_colour(minimum, maximum):
15      red=random.randint(minimum,maximum)
16      green=random.randint(minimum,maximum)
17      blue=random.randint(minimum,maximum)
18      colour=[red,green,blue]
19      return colour
20
21  for n in range(100):
22      clock.tick(25)
23      colour=random_colour(100,255)
24      draw_circle(colour)
25      pygame.display.update()
26
27  raw_input("Press a key")
```

Python indentation makes it easy to see which code is part of which block

The basics

Python is what's known as an *interpreted* language. This means that when you want to run a program you've written, it must be saved as a text file and passed to another program called the Python Interpreter, which reads in your code and converts it, on a line-by-line basis, into low-level code that the computer understands. You can contrast this with C, which is a *compiled* language: with C, before your code can be run, it's entirely converted into a machine-readable form that doesn't need an interpreter.

All things being equal, compiled code runs more quickly than its interpreted equivalent, because it's ready to go when it's loaded; Python needs to first load its runtime engine – that is, the software the PC needs to run to convert the language from high level to low level – and then read in the text files and then, finally, run the program.

You might wonder why, in that case, we have interpreted languages. First, because the difference in speed is, for most real-world purposes, undetectable on modern hardware (even the Raspberry Pi). Sure, if you wanted to create a 3D engine for a first-person video game, you'd write it in C (or C++) rather than Python to get the best possible performance, but most games – and most other programs – run perfectly through a runtime engine.

Another important benefit of an interpreted language is that it eliminates a step from the development process. With Python you can write code, save it and immediately run it to see whether it works. With C, you must write, save and compile before you get results. The more code you write, the longer this process takes and the more time you save with Python.

We've described in the last chapter how the work a computer program does can be divided into input, logic and output processes. In practice, this means that Python programs tend to be made up of several text files that are usually saved with a .py extension. In most cases there is a central file, normally called main.py, which is the starting point: this is the text file that the interpreter is instructed to run.

The other files are linked to main.py using the **import** statement and, if you could slow down the interpreter to human reading speed, you'd be able to watch as it jumps in and out of those other files in response to your commands, but always returning back to main.py. Geany makes all this simple because it has a button on the toolbar for running the project – just make sure you have main.py in the edit window when you click!

The Python philosophy

Very few programmers stick to a single language, and as you gain experience of programming, you'll notice that different languages seem to have "personalities" of their own. Quite often, you'll find you come to prefer one language over another because its personality appeals to you – so it's good news that Python is easy to like.

As you'd expect from a language that takes its name from a TV comedy series, Python doesn't take itself too seriously. Some languages seem to hoard their secrets and so attract fans who take great pride in overcoming their limitations: the harder it is to get something done, the more they seem to like it. Python takes the opposite approach and this has helped to build a community of fans eager to help others get into the language.

The Zen of Python

1. **There is one right way to do it.** Some languages encourage you to find your own way of achieving something, providing many different methods. Whilst Python has plenty of flexibility when it comes to organising your code (which is your business), when it comes to writing individual lines of code to carry out a task there's usually a single best way to go about it. If it feels as though you're going around the houses to get something done, there's almost certainly a better way.

2. **Always choose simple over complex and complex over complicated.** Python is built to make it easy for you to write simple code. This is good because it reduces bugs and makes it simpler to maintain your program – whether you're doing it or someone else. If you can't make it simple then make it complex, but keep it clear rather than complicated.

3. **Get it done.** Python is an incredibly productive language. It takes a remarkably small amount of code to achieve useful results. Whereas programmers using other languages boast about how many lines of code their application contains, Python programmers brag about how few lines it took.

4. **Organise for readability.** As we'll see, Python includes many ways of putting code into blocks to get things done. You can also put blocks within blocks (within blocks) but this leads to code that's difficult to understand. If this happens when writing Python code, think about how you can put the sub-blocks elsewhere (into modules, functions or objects for example) so that the main code remains simple to read.

5. **Have fun.** Whereas coding in some languages can feel as though you're wading through treacle to do the simplest things – Objective-C and Java, I'm looking at you – using Python is a joy. If you don't have fun writing programs using Python then you might want to reconsider taking up programming. As with any new skill learning to program is a challenge, but Python makes it as simple as possible whilst doing its best to demand little and deliver plenty.

▶ **Focus On** ▶ **No curly braces**

If you've seen programming code at any point, you've probably seen curly braces used to divide code into blocks. When the interpreter reaches an opening curly brace – "{" – it knows that everything that follows belongs together, until it gets to a closing brace. The problem with this approach is that you end up with a lot of curly braces!

Traditionally, programmers have used tab indenting to make a visual link: in other words, all the code that's indented by one tab stop belongs together. However, most languages use the braces to group code, so using tab stops is purely optional and anything that's optional tends to get forgotten by busy programmers. The end result is a mess of braces that can be very difficult to understand.

Python solves this problem by not using curly braces at all, but relying entirely on indentation. In other words, if you don't organise your code to be easy to read, it won't work; but code that does work, by definition, is readable. Remember, then, to take care with indenting. It becomes natural very quickly but it's also the biggest single source of errors by new coders, especially those transferring across from another language.

Python basics: statements and expressions

We've looked at how programs are split, like a book, into smaller and smaller subdivisions. When you're planning a novel, you need to think about the overall plot, character and setting – but actually writing the book is done one word at a time, building up sentences, paragraphs, pages and chapters. Planning a program involves thinking about what you want to achieve through input-logic-output and how that's reflected in its modules, objects and functions, but it boils down to typing code letter by letter into an editor.

The programming equivalent of the sentence is a *statement* – the smallest chunk of code that makes sense on its own. Statements are usually made up of several expressions, which are similar to verbs in that they get things done. They achieve this by creating and using *objects*, whether these are built into Python or created separately (perhaps by you).

One of the main advantages of Python over lower-level languages is the range of pre-existing objects you can draw upon. If you were a C programmer you'd spend much of your time manually setting up objects; using Python allows you to bypass much of this and get on with making something useful quickly.

Start up Geany

We're going to look at some simple code, and the best possible way for you to learn is to follow along. To do this, start up Geany and click the Terminal tab in the Message window at the bottom. If you don't see the Message window, click the View menu, and select "Show Message Window" option. If Terminal is not amongst the tabs and you're using Linux, then open up a terminal window and type the following line to install it.

```
sudo apt-get install libvte9
```

Now, restart Geany and the tab should appear. If it doesn't then use LXTerminal (on the Raspberry Pi) or the Terminal app in other forms of Linux. If you're using Windows, you'll need to run the command prompt.

In all cases, now type "python" into the Terminal tab (or window) to start the Python interpreter. You should get a message reporting which version of Python is running, followed by the prompt >>>, which indicates that it's waiting for input. What's happening here is that you are talking directly to the interpreter rather than loading a text file into it. This means you can try things out instantly, which is what we're going to do now.

Note: in the code snippets that follow, if we want you to type code into the interpreter via the terminal/command prompt, we'll start the line with >>>. Lines that don't begin with the chevrons represent text the interpreter is "printing" out and should not be typed.

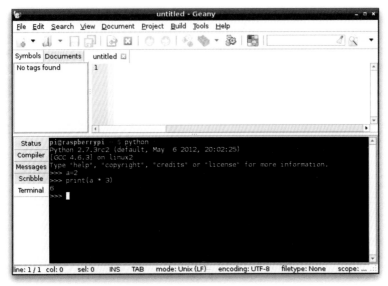

It's easy to explore how variables work in Python using Geany's Terminal tab

Variables

In basic algebra, you swap numbers for letters to help solve problems. For example:

$$a \times 3 = 6$$

In this case, a is equal to 2. Variables work in a similar way – they act as containers for values. These values can be numbers, letters or even objects – the variable works as a convenient way of working on a value and passing it from place to place.

Let's look at this by re-writing the above code as it might appear in a real program. Go to the Terminal tab in Geany (or a running terminal or command prompt) and type the following lines, pressing Enter after each (don't type the chevrons!):

```
>>> a=2
>>> print(a * 3)
6
```

The first line creates a variable called a and gives it a value of 2. The second line is a *statement* that contains an object (`print`) and an expression (a * 3). What makes the last part an expression is that it returns a value that it has calculated. In this case, Python multiplies the variable a (which contains a value of 2 as set in the previous line) by 3 giving a result of 6. Note that in programming, we use the asterisk to indicate multiplication.

The result is sent to the print object which, as you'll have guessed already, simply writes the value to the message window. You should see the number appear on the next line.

Here's a variation:

```
>>> a = 2
>>> b = 3
>>> print(a * b)
6
```

You'll see the number 6 appear again, just as before. This time two variables were multiplied together.

Let's try a simple VAT calculator. Type the following and press Enter:

```
>>>beforeVAT=raw_input("Add VAT to this: ")
```

raw_input is a Python function that asks the user to type something in. In this case, we add a message asking them to tell us what figure they want us to add VAT to. This figure is then assigned to the variable beforeVAT.

When you see the prompt, type a number (for example, 100) and press Enter. Then type the following, pressing Enter after each line:

```
>>>afterVAT=float(beforeVAT)*1.2
>>>print(afterVAT)
```

The second line creates a new variable, afterVAT, which is the result of beforeVAT (the number you typed in) multiplied by 1.2 (which has the effect of adding 20%) and, finally, we print this new value out on the next line.

```
pi@raspberrypi ~ $ python
Python 2.7.3rc2 (default, May  6 2012, 20:02:25)
[GCC 4.6.3] on linux2
Type "help", "copyright", "credits" or "license" for more information.
>>> beforeVAT=raw_input("Add VAT to this: ")
Add VAT to this: 100
>>> afterVAT=float(beforeVAT)*1.2
>>> print(afterVAT)
120.0
>>>
```

It's possible to carry out some quite sophisticated calculations in Terminal view, so you can try out different mathematical operations

Now, that's all very well but what if we wanted to use this program again? Commands typed into the interpreter will be erased from memory when you shut down your computer or Geany; we're going to start creating files for our programs so we can keep and reuse them.

In Geany, select File | New (don't select a template) and type the following line (including the # symbol)

```
#my first program
```

Now save the file to a location of your choice, making sure you add the extension .py to the end of the file name. You should notice that your single line has turned red. This is because any line that begins with the # symbol is ignored by Python – it's used to make comments in your code so that when you come back to it you can understand what you were doing. Geany knows you're writing Python code because you added .py to the file name, so it's turned the line red to indicate a comment.

Retype all the lines of the VAT calculator into Geany. Notice that, as you type the first few characters of raw_input, Geany offers an autocomplete – press Enter to accept. It also shows you what information raw_input expects you to type in – this can be useful to help you learn the specific commands and also reduces bugs.

Once you've typed each line, save the file and then click the Execute button on the Geany toolbar (the cogs). After a short delay, LXTerminal will pop up and your prompt will appear. Type a number and Python will tell you what the total including VAT would be.

Now that the program has been saved, you can run it as many times as you like by loading it into Geany and clicking Execute.

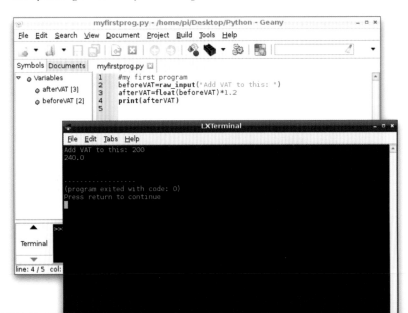

▶ **Focus On** ▶ **Variable names**

You have plenty of flexibility about what you call your variables. You can use any letter and number (although the first character of a variable can't be a number – "1ucy" is invalid, for example) and also the underscore character. There are a few words that Python uses itself, such as "else", which you can't use. Don't worry too much, though, it will soon tell you!

The Python community uses some conventions which, in the main, we'll follow in this book. In the end, however, whatever system you use needs to make sense to you. You can't use spaces in variable names as they must all be one word.

One way to get around this is to use the underscore character; another is to capitalise the first letter of words after the first – this is called camelCase. It's up to you whether you believe that `my_variable` is a better name than `myvariable`; Python doesn't mind – both are more readable than `myvariable` though. For now, just try to be consistent.

Data

We've seen that we can use variables as containers and then do things with them. We've used numbers in the example so far, but Python provides several types that you'll be using a lot. Here are the most important:

Numbers

Which of the following are numbers?

3290, 3290.123, 3290e3, "3290"

We can find out by making use of the fact that Python is a *strongly typed* language. This means that if you try to multiply two variables that aren't both numbers, for example, it will report an error. PHP, which is another popular programming language, would do its best to work out what you meant – but this can often result in bugs. Go back to the Geany Terminal tab and type:

```
>>> a=3290; print(a*5)
16450
```

Python prints the answer we'd expect. Notice that semi-colon? It's there to allow us to put two statements on one line. Other languages use the semi-colon at the end of every line. In Python, we use it only when we want to use multiple statements on a single line.

Now let's try the next one:

```
>>> a=3290.123; print(a*5)
16450.615
```

This time, the number has a decimal point – in Python, numbers formatted in this way are called *floats,* because they have a floating decimal point. Numbers without points are called *integers.* Floats take up a little more memory than integers, so use them only if you need the extra precision. Note that when two number types are multiplied (the floating point 3290.123 and the integer 5), Python shows the answer in the most precise form – in this case, as a float.

Back to the terminal:

```
>>>a=3290e3; print(a*5)
16450000.0
```

This is another type of floating point number, except that this time we used e3 at the end: this is a convenient way of signifying 3,290 x 10^3 or, to put it another way, 3,290,000.

Now try:

```
>>>a="3290"; print(a*5)
32903290329032903290
```

That was unexpected! But completely logical – to Python. By putting quotes around the number, you told Python that the characters 3290 were intended to be treated as a *string* rather than a number. A string is a sequence of letters, numbers and symbols intended to be treated as text. When you multiply a string, as we did here, Python thinks you want multiple copies so it just repeats them.

To see Python throw a real wobbler, try this slightly different version (with a plus rather than a multiplication symbol):

```
>>>a="3290"; print(a+5)
```

What happens? Python shows an error message. This is because the + symbol is interpreted in different ways depending on whether it's dealing with numbers – where it means to add the numbers together arithmetically – or strings, where it means glue the second onto the end of the first. So, `"raspberry" + "pi"` becomes `"raspberry pi"`; but faced with the expression `"raspberry" +` 3.141592 (the number pi), Python is unable to perform the operation and will simply return an error.

Although Python has several other number types, most of the time you'll stick to integers and floats. As you've seen, to perform arithmetic on numbers, we use the * *operator* to represent "multiplied by" and + to indicate addition. We can also process numbers in different ways using built-in functions and modules – the most useful being the `math` module.

We'll come across all of these later but, as a taster, here's a list of the main operators and functions you'll come across:

Operator/function	What it does	Example
+	Numerical addition	`>>> a=9; b=a+5; print b` `14`
-	Numerical subtraction	`>>> a=9; b=a-5; print b` `4`
*	Multiply by	`>>> a=9; b=a*5; print b` `45`
/	Divided by	`>>> a=9.0; b=a/5; print b` `1.8`
%	Modulus (the remainder of a division)	`>>> a=9; b=a%5; print b` `4`

int	Convert to an integer	`>>>a=9.0; b=a/5; print`
		`int(b)`
		`1`

round	Round to the nearest float	`>>>a=9.0; b=a/5; print`
		`round(b)`
		`2.0`

float	Convert to a float	`>>>a=9; b=float(a)/5; print b` `1.8`

Of these, modulus is probably the only one that's not immediately obvious. That's partly because the percentage sign is commonly used to mean something quite different. The term may also be unfamiliar: it simply means the remainder that's left after performing a division. So, 11%2 gives a result of 1, because 2 goes into 11 five times with 1 left over.

You'd be surprised at how often this is used in programming: it's excellent for finding out if a number is odd or even, because any even number divided by 2 will have a modulus of 0, whereas any odd number divided by 2 always results in a modulus of 1. You might use this when shading the rows of a table alternately, for example.

The math module includes some additional useful and interesting functions, too. Python has two types of built-in function: those such as round that can be used as if they were part of the language; and those such as `math.floor` that can only be used if the appropriate module is imported first. Don't worry, it's very simple – take a look at these. Remember, they're still all one line:

Function	What it does	Example
math.floor	Always rounds down to the nearest integer	```>>>import math; a=9.0; b=a/5; print math.floor(b) 1.0```
math.ceil	Always rounds up to the nearest integer	```>>>import math; a=9.0; b=a/5; print math.ceil(b) 2.0```
math.pi	Stores the value of pi	```>>>import math; print math.pi 3.14159265359```

Strings
String variables are used to store things such as usernames, text we're going to display on-screen (for example, the prompt we used earlier with raw_input), and other elements we might want to work with, such as database entries. To tell Python you want a variable to be a string, you can enclose the text in either double or single quotes – it makes no difference from the interpreter's point of view. These are equally valid:

```
>>>myName="Terry"
>>>myName='Terry'
```

The only thing you need to look out for is to use the same marks at the start and end of the string. If you try to use double quotes at the start and single at the end, Python will return an error. If the phrase itself includes speech marks or apostrophes, simply use the other punctuation mark to enclose it:

```
>>>myName="Terry's Terrifics"
>>>myName='Terry "Terrific" Travis"
```

▶ **Focus On** It's maths – but don't panic!!

If the idea of having to deal with maths brings you out in a cold sweat, there's good news. Far from being the difficult-to-grasp subject you might have found it at school, maths is at the heart of all computer programming, so you'll get to see its practical use. Plus, the vast majority of the maths-related programming you'll ever have to do is based on simple arithmetic.

In other words, if the string contains apostrophes, you simply need to surround it with double quotes, and vice versa. Given that apostrophes and single quotes turn up in text more often than speech marks, it makes sense to use double quotes by default.

Hold on – what if a piece of text contains both? In this case, simply add a backslash in front of the character you've used to enclose the string where it appears within the text. This tells Python that the character is to be taken literally. For example, here's how we might signal to Python that the internal apostrophe in a phrase is to be treated as part of our string, and not as an end-marker:

```
>>>myName='Terry\'s the "Terrific" Travis'
```

Things to do with strings
Once you've loaded some text into your variable to create a string, Python allows you to process it in all sorts of weird and wonderful ways. Python thinks of strings as being similar to Scrabble tiles – each character on its own tile – which makes it really easy to get at any letter or number, as well as dead simple to split the string into bits. There are dozens of functions designed to handle strings, but the selection below will give you an idea of how such functions work and how they might be used:

Function	What it does	Example
len	Tells us how long a string is (including spaces)	`>>>print len("Terry Travis")` `12`
+	Add (concatenate) two strings together	`>>>print "Terry " + "Travis"` `Terry Travis`
String[position]	Return the character at that position in the string (the first position is zero)	`>>>a="Terry Travis"; print a[0]` `T`
String[p1:p2]	Return all the characters between two positions	`>>>a="Terry Travis"; print a[5:12]` `Travis`
replace(old,new)	Replaces an existing set of characters with another	`>>>a="Terry Travis"; print a.replace("rav","ard")` `Terry Tardis`
split	Splits a string into parts	`>>>a="Terry Travis"; print a.split()` `['Terry', 'Travis']`

Lists

Strings and numbers contain single values: Python's list object lets you store multiple values in one variable. Imagine, for example, you had a database of names such as "Terry Travis" and you wanted to write to everyone using their first name only. The names could be stored in a list object, then pulled out one at a time so that the split() function could be used to fetch the first name from each.

Here's how we might define that list of names. Note that because the line is longer than our margins can accommodate, we've used the symbol "▶" to indicate that the code spills over to the next line. Don't press Return when you see this symbol, but keep typing to the end of the next line.

```
>>>list_of_names=['Andrew Ant','Charlie Childs','Martina ▶
Mongoose','Peter Purbrook','Terry Travis','Vera Verity']
```

Once this list is entered, to pull out Terry we could do this:

```
>>>this_name=list_of_names[4]
>>>print "Full name="+this_name
Full name=Terry Travis
```

To isolate just his first name:

```
>>>first_name=this_name.split()[0]
>>>print "First name="+first_name
First name=Terry
```

In Python – and most other computer languages – when you're selecting elements from inside a variable, the numbering starts with 0, not 1 as you might expect. This number is called an *index* and the item it fetches is called an *element*.

In the case of a string, specifying a single index gives you one character from the string as its element; with a list, you get the whole element. So, "Terry Travis"[0] would return "T" (the first character) whereas list_of_names[0] would give you "Andrew Ant".

A list can contain a mix of variables, including other lists. For example, for a calendar divided into the weeks of the year, each week could be a list containing the dates. This is how that would look for the beginning of 2013:

```
>>>year_2013=[[31,1,2,3,4,5,6],[7,8,9,10,11,12,13],[14,15,16, ▶
17,18,19,20],[21,22,23,24,25,26,27],[28,29,30,31,1,2,3]]
>>>week=year_2013[1]
>>>print week
[7, 8, 9, 10, 11, 12, 13]
```

Note how each of the *nested* lists is contained within square brackets. The second line fetches the dates for the second week in January (remember, list indexes start with 0); that is, a list within a list. You could extract the date for Wednesday of that week with `week[2]`.

As you can see, lists allow you to pack a lot of data into a single variable. Don't worry if they seem a little complex right now. We'll be using lists a lot and you'll soon get to grips with them.

Dictionaries

You can think of dictionaries as super-lists. Like lists, they're collections of other objects; unlike lists, each element is given its own name so you can access the variable directly. Try this:

```
>>> family={'father':'Terry', 'mother':'Vera', ►
'daughter':'Jane', 'son':'Jack'}
>>> print family['father']
Terry
```

As you can see, each pair is given a name and a value. We can then pull out any dictionary element by using that name. As you'd expect, this means that each name must be used only once per dictionary. You'll also notice that dictionaries use curly braces to indicate when they start and end, whereas lists use square brackets – this is how Python knows which of the two you mean to create.

You can change the contents of both lists and dictionaries during a program. If you typed in the family example above, you could change it like this:

```
>>>family['son']='Jak'
>>>print family['son']
Jak
```

You don't have to use *literal* values when you create a dictionary or list – you can use a variable instead.

```
>>>son="Jake"
>>>family['son']=son
>>>print family['son']
Jake
```

This time, we created a new variable called `son` and assigned it a string value "Jake". We can then use the variable to feed into the family dictionary. Not particularly useful as it stands, but imagine if we were reading a database of families: we'd then be able to change the son variable to the name of each son without having to type them manually. A final useful thing to know is that you can add a new entry to a dictionary after it's been created. In this case, let's add grandparents:

```
>>>family['grandad']='Cyril'
>>>family['granny']='Edith'
>>>print family
{'daughter': 'Jane', 'grandad': 'Cyril', 'mother': 'Vera', ▶
'father': 'Terry', 'son': 'Jake', 'granny': 'Edith'}
```

▶ Focus On ▶ Arrays

If you've ever used another programming language, you'll probably have come across *arrays*. In that case, you may have already worked out that *lists* and *dictionaries* are the equivalent Python structures. Where you might have used a standard array sorted by index in PHP, for example, you use the *list* in Python. *Dictionaries* are the equivalent of *associative arrays* in other languages. If you've never programmed before, just bear this in mind when you look at the documentation for other languages – this is one aspect in which Python is quite unusual.

Fortune teller

Remember those little plastic balls that presented a random answer to your questions when you shook them? Let's create our own fortune teller in Python – in just a few lines of code. We're going to want to run this more than once, so fire up Geany and type in the listing. Remember that the ▶ on line 2 tells you to keep typing, rather than pressing Return to start a new line.

```
import random
fortunes=['Yes','Probably','Certainly','Outlook promising', ▶
'Not sure','Ask again','Doubtful','No']
how_many_fortunes=len(fortunes)
raw_input('Think of a question, press Enter for the answer')
which_fortune=random.randint(0,how_many_fortunes-1)
print fortunes[which_fortune]
```

The code begins by importing the `random` module, which will produce the random numbers that allow us to pick an unpredictable answer each time the program is run. On the following line we create a list containing all eight of the possible answers – feel free to change them as you wish!

On the next line we use the `len` function to find out how many answers there are. This might seem unnecessary because we could simply count them (`how_many_fortunes=8`), but by doing it this way we can add and remove answers at any point without affecting the rest of the code.

The following line uses the `raw_input` statement to pause the program, displays the prompt and waits for the user to press the Enter key.

Next, we use the `randint` function to generate a number. Notice the brackets after `randint`? Those are there to pass *parameters* to randint. Parameters are the bits of information the function needs to work. In this case, we're telling randint to generate a number between 0 and `how_many_fortunes-1`. Given that there are eight fortunes in our example, this means `randint` will give us a number between zero and seven. We need this because, in case you've forgotten, the first item in a list has an index of 0, not 1 as you might expect. Therefore, the last one has an index of 7, not 8. Don't worry if you find this a little frustrating: the zero-based indexing of lists and other similar objects catches out the most experienced programmers from time to time.

Finally, on the last line of the program, we print the element from `fortunes` that has the index generated by `randint`.

Run the program a couple of times by clicking the cogs to make sure the randomness is working; you should receive a different answer pretty much every time (though it's to be expected that things will repeat occasionally – that's the nature of randomness). Also have a go at changing the text in the answers and adding or removing some.

Congratulations! You have just written your most advanced computer program yet – a fortune-telling genie, in only six lines of code!

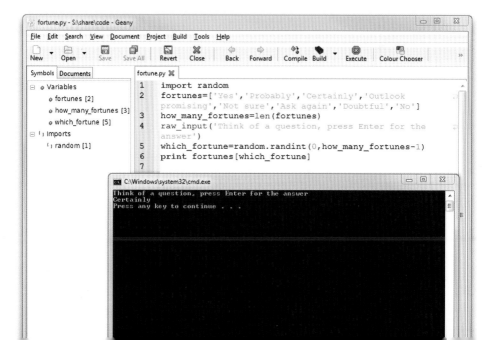

Making decisions and getting things done

Image: Steve Kimberley (http://en.wikipedia.org/wiki/File:Loom.jpg)

A loom powered by punched cards in modern-day use in India

Over 200 years ago, Joseph Jacquard demonstrated a new mechanical loom with a unique feature: it used punched cards to control the pattern of the textile. Each card contained several rows of holes in specific locations. As the card was fed through, row by row, small rods detected whether there was a hole. If there was, that particular thread would be used; if not, it wouldn't.

Since each row in Jacquard's system offered 25-30 positions for holes, very complex patterns could be created with minimal human involvement. Loading up another set of cards yielded a completely different pattern.

This invention (building on earlier work by others) was such an efficient way to create textiles that it's still in wide use today. It also gave rise to two important concepts that formed the foundation of computing: the idea that you can program a series of operations in advance and, secondly, that a machine can be given more than one purpose by simply changing its "software" (or "paperware" in this case).

Another similarity between Jacquard's system and modern computing becomes apparent if you take one row from a set of Jacquard cards, and represent a hole with a 1 and the absence of a hole with 0. You might get a sequence like this: 111110011000001100111001111111. In other words, Jacquard used a 19th-century implementation of binary notation – the "language" at the heart of all digital computers. The looms used mechanics in place of programming languages but, essentially, they worked in a similar way. If a 1 was encountered in any particular position, a certain action was taken; if it wasn't then either a different action was taken or nothing happened.

Jacquard's system had only one variable type (a binary number), whereas Python has many (including its equivalent of the binary type, namely the Boolean). We've covered the most important of these – numbers, strings, lists and dictionaries. Now it's time to move onto the coding equivalent of the mechanics that decide what to do with those variables.

If-then-else

The ability to make decisions based on the contents of variables and then take actions depending on the results is what separates computers from calculators, and *if-then-else* is the most important decision-making structure. In the case of the Jacquard loom, each position on the card where there might be a hole is a simple if-statement. In English, this could be written as:

```
If there's a hole here use blue thread,
otherwise use yellow thread.
```

In Python, that statement might be represented as:

```
if hole==1:
    thread=blue
else:
    thread=yellow
```

The first thing you'll notice is how clear this code is – we mentioned in chapter 2 how easy Python is to understand – and this sort of readability is one of the main aims of the language. We begin with the if keyword, and we follow this with the *condition* that's being tested.

In this case, if the hole variable (a number) is equal to 1 then the program moves immediately to the next line. You'll notice that this line is indented and Python will now carry out all lines at that indentation (in this case, there is only one). If the hole variable is *not* 1 then the interpreter skips down to the line containing else and executes the code beneath it.

Python uses a colon to indicate the start of a block of code and then continues until the indentation changes. In practice what this means is that you add the colon, then hit the Enter key to start a new line. You then hit tab once (Geany does this automatically after a colon) and type your first line – every other line that's also tabbed once will be executed one after another. The interpreter will stop when it spots a different indentation.

This is really important – Python is the only mainstream language that relies entirely on indentation to mark blocks of code. The benefit of this is that your code is much clearer, as we explained earlier, but it takes a little getting used to. Let's look at a slightly more involved chunk of code to help you understand. Don't type in the line numbers – these are just for our reference. We've also left some blank lines and colour-coded the different sections of this program, to help you follow the structure.

```
1    input_name=raw_input("What is your name?")
2    name_length=len(input_name)
3    average_name_length=5
4
5    if name_length>average_name_length:
6        result="longer"
7        conjunction="than"
8    elif name_length<average_name_length:
9        result="shorter"
10       conjunction="than"
11   else:
12       result="the same"
13       conjunction="length as"
14
15   response=input_name+", your name is "+result+" ▶
         "+conjunction+" "+"average"
16   print response
```

This program asks the user to type in their name. It then works out how many characters their name contains. The `if` block compares this with the average length of a first name (the `average_name_length` variable) and puts together a response depending on the result.

At line 5 – the start of the red section – the length of the user's name is compared to the average. If their name length is *greater* than the average (we use the mathematical > symbol), then the following code in red is carried out. Once Python reaches the end of the red text, it jumps out of the `if` statement and straight down to line 15.

If their name length is not greater than average, the interpreter skips the red text and then evaluates line 8. `elif` is short for "else if" – in other words, "now check whether this is true". Here, we ask if their name length is *less than* (<) the average. If it is, the code in blue is carried out, then Python jumps to line 15.

If the user's name is neither larger nor smaller than the average, it must be the same length. So, we use `else` as a catch-all: it means "if none of the others is true, then do this". Note that Python will only arrive at this line if it hasn't already been diverted by one of the other if statements. This time it will carry out the instructions in green before jumping to line 15. Give it a try with names of different lengths to make sure it works.

We've now met three different ways to compare two variables: equals (==), less than (<) and greater than (>). The complete list of commonly used *comparison operators* is shown here:

Operator	What does it do?	Example
==	Are the two values **the same**?	if a==b:
<	Is the first value **less than** the second?	if a<b:
>	Is the first value **more than** the second?	if a>b:
>=	Is the first value **greater than or equal** to the second?	if a>=b:
<=	Is the first value **less than or equal to** the second?	if a<=b:
!= or <>	Is the first value **not equal** to the second?	if a!=b:

In other words, when used in an if statement, if the answer to the question is *yes* then Python executes the code immediately following. If not, it skips to the next block. Finally, in case you were wondering, we use == rather than = for "equals" in conditional statements because Python assigns values to variables using =. Watch out for this – it'll trip you up sooner or later!

Repeating yourself

Using only *if-then-else* structures leads to very short programs. Remember our fortune teller app? Every time you wanted to ask a new question, you were forced to run the program again. The Jacquard Loom, conversely, kept on going because the cards were constantly fed into the machine via a loop mechanism; otherwise it would have only created one line of thread.

Similarly, we can create loops in our programs, to run sections of code multiple times. Almost every useful Python program will include loops.

For..in

If you want to do something a specific number of times, the for loop is the tool to pick. Let's take a look at a very simple for loop in action:

```
input_name=raw_input("What is your name?")
for c in input_name:
    print c
```

Give it a go. Create a Python file in Geany, type in those three lines and run it. When prompted, enter your name. You'll find that Python then prints each character of your name one at a time, each on a separate line.

The structure of a `for` loop is this:

```
for [iterator] in [collection]:
```

Collection means any variable that can be split into parts. Lists and dictionaries are often used but, in this example, it's a string. *Iterator* is just the name we give to each bit as it's pulled out. Put into English, our example would be "for each letter in input_name", and it means that the next line will be repeated until it gets to the end of the collection (the name you typed in, in this example).

So, let's say you typed "Jo Bloggs" at the prompt. Collection is therefore "Jo Bloggs" and the loop will start. The value of our iterator will be "J" to begin with and so the print line will output that letter. Python now checks to see if we've reached the end of the collection and, since we haven't, moves to the next letter and prints "o". Bear in mind that if there were several lines after the `for` statement, Python would execute them all as part of the loop – until it got to a line that wasn't in the same tab position, at which point it would go back to the `for` and start again.

What do you think would happen if you were to replace the first line with the code below? Give it a try.

```
input_name=("Jo", "Bloggs")
```

You should find that, this time, Python prints "Jo" on one line and "Bloggs" on the next, rather than each word on its own line. Why? Because `input_name` is now a list, not a string, so the iterator is now each element in the list, not the individual characters in the string. In fact, it's much more common to iterate over a list than a string, largely because lists are so useful.

If you've studied any other programming language, you've probably come across a `for` structure that iterates a fixed number of times. In BASIC this would be written as `for n=1 to 10`, which would create a loop that ran ten times. Whilst this might seem simpler, in practice you nearly always iterate through a collection, so the Python approach is much more efficient. If you do need to loop a fixed number of times – for example, if you wanted to create a specific number of objects – the Python equivalent of that BASIC statement would be:

```
for n in range(10):
```

Again, below this statement, simply place the code you want to be run ten times (in this case), indented by one tab stop.

While

Most Python programs, especially games, include the `while` loop. In English, this loop means "while a particular condition is satisfied, keep looping". For example, in a game you'll usually have a main loop that keeps repeating until the Escape key is pressed:

```
import random
user_roll=raw_input("What number did you roll?")
my_roll=0
how_many_rolls=0

while my_roll != int(user_roll):
    my_roll=random.randint(1,6)
    how_many_rolls+=1
    print my_roll

print "it took "+str(how_many_rolls)+" rolls"
```

This little program asks you to roll a die and input the number. It then works out how many rolls it took to get the same number (on average it should be around six). As you can see, we need to begin by importing the `random` module. We also create two number variables and set them to zero.

When Python gets to the `while` loop, it checks its value for `my_roll` (remember, we set it to zero when we created it) and compares that to the number you entered. The `!=` comparison means "does not equal" so, if `my_roll` does **not** equal the user's number then Python will move into the block. Since you will have typed a number from one to six, `my_roll` will not equal `user_roll` the first time, so Python will always run the loop at least once.

We then set `my_roll` to a randomly generated number between one and six to simulate our die roll. On the next line we increase the `how_many_rolls` variable by one to keep track of the number of rolls it took to get the same number the user rolled. The `+=` characters are used as a shorthand to increase (*increment*) that value by one.

We then print the randomly generated die roll, and Python jumps back to the `while` line. This time `my_roll` will not be zero, it will be a number from one to six. Python checks whether this randomly generated number matches whatever the user typed in earlier. If it doesn't, it moves into the loop again. This continues until they do match, each time generating and printing out a new random number. When it does match, Python jumps to the final line and prints out the number of attempts it took.

You'll notice that the `while` statement includes the `int` function. This is because, when we use `raw_input`, the user's input is treated as a string, even if they've typed in numbers. Python can't compare a number with a string (even if that string contains only digits), so we use the int function to convert the string into an integer (a number without a decimal point) that the while statement can use to compare. Similarly, on the final line, we use the str function to turn the how_many_rolls number variable into a string so it can be incorporated into the print statement.

Decisions, loops, nesting and breaks

Loops and *if-then-else* structures are at their most powerful when they work together. You can also create loops within loops (this is called *nesting*) and ifs within ifs – and any combination of both. Indeed, a program of any complexity at all will involve these sorts of combinations and it can be tricky to work out where you are at any one time.

But this is where Python's clear structure pays off: you know that all lines at the same tab stop are at the same level. This is much easier than the approach other languages use of employing curly braces – in that case, unless you've been hyper-careful making sure your tabs line up, you'll end up counting braces to see where you are. In Python, if you don't line up your tabs, the program won't work so you're forced to get it right. This is a good thing!

Occasionally, you will want to break out of a loop before it has completed. If you'd created a Space Invaders-type game, for example, and were using a while loop to update the position of the invaders several times a second, you might want to exit to another part of the program if the user pressed F1 for help. In that case, you use the **break** statement; this exits the loop immediately and proceeds as if it had completed.

The **continue** statement, on the other hand, skips straight back to the start of the loop, preventing Python from executing the remaining lines in that cycle.

Organising your code: functions, objects and modules

We've covered Python's most important nuts and bolts – variables, decisions and loops – enough to create simple programs. However, to create a useful application, you need a way to organise your code. Otherwise it would end up as one long, indecipherable block of Python.

Going back to our book analogy, functions are the equivalent of paragraphs: a chunk of lines with a specific purpose. Functions can exist on their own or within objects or modules. They're the smallest unit in the Python universe.

Functions

A function is a block of code with a particular purpose. By organising your code this way, it can be used as many times as you like from within your program. For example, you might have a function that reads the system clock every second to update the elapsed time in a game. Rather than having several lines of code to do this within the main program, this can be isolated into a function to be called as often as you like. This has the added benefit of making our main code much simpler and easier to understand because it isn't so cluttered. Each function can be named, which, again, makes the program as a whole much easier to understand.

Let's get straight into a practical example. Type the listing below into Geany and run it.

```
1    import pygame,random
2    pygame.init()
3    clock = pygame.time.Clock() # Clock to limit speed
4    WIDTH=600; HEIGHT=600; BLACK=(0,0,0)
5    screen = pygame.display.set_mode([WIDTH, HEIGHT])
6    screen.fill(BLACK)
7
8    def draw_circle(colour):
9        x=random.randint(1,WIDTH)
10       y=random.randint(1,HEIGHT)
11       size=random.randint(1,5)
12       pygame.draw.circle(screen,colour,(x,y),size)
13
14   def random_colour(minimum, maximum):
15       red=random.randint(minimum,maximum)
16       green=random.randint(minimum,maximum)
17       blue=random.randint(minimum,maximum)
18       colour=[red,green,blue]
19       return colour
20
21   for n in range(100):
22       clock.tick(25)
23       colour=random_colour(100,255)
24       draw_circle(colour)
25       pygame.display.update()
26
27   raw_input("Press a key")
```

This simple program fills a black window with randomly generated circles. You'll remember that when we created if-then-else, while and for..in blocks, we started the block with a colon and then indented the code that is to be run. Functions work in exactly the same way.

We use the def keyword to **def**ine a function. You can see that, in this code,

we have two functions, which we've called
draw_circle and random_colour – we
can use any name that makes sense to us
and follows the rules for naming variables.

When the program is run, Python
will begin at line 1 and immediately carry
out the instructions through to line 6
(note the two variables WIDTH and HEIGHT
are in capitals – this is the convention
for variables whose values stay the same
throughout. When it gets to line 8, it
comes across the first function: rather
than being immediately run, the code
within the function is loaded into memory
to be used later. The same happens with
the second function (random_color).

The Python interpreter arrives at line
21 and finds a for..in loop. In this case,
it's a loop that will run exactly a hundred
times, since this is how many circles we

Our randomly generated circles are attractive
to look at, and were easy to implement

want to generate. In other words, Python carries out the code from line 22 to line
25 one hundred times before the loop ends. The interpreter then jumps down to
line 27, which waits for a key to be pressed before ending the program.

To run the code in a function, we **call** it – you can see the two ways to do
this on lines 23 and 24. The purpose of many functions is to carry out a task and
send back the result. Take a wild guess at what line 23 is doing:

```
colour=random_colour(100,255)
```

Yes, we're creating a variable called colour and assigning it the value sent
back by the function random_colour. Note that every single element in this
statement was named by us, not Python, so we can choose words that make
sense to us so that our code is easy to understand.

But what about the set of brackets at the end? Well, have a look at the
function definition on line 14. Immediately after we name the function, we also
indicate what information the function needs in order to run: in other words,
which *parameters* must be passed to it. In this case, we need a minimum and
maximum value for the colour (see *Focus on: Colour* for an explanation of how
colour works in Python).

Since our background window is black, we don't want colours that are too
dark. Look back at line 23 and you'll see we're passing 100 to the function as the
first parameter (minimum) and 255 as the second parameter (maximum).

Each of the first three lines of this function (starting at line 14) generates a random number between `minimum` and `maximum` (100 to 255 in this case). The variable names have been chosen to make clear what they represent. However, `red`, `green` and `blue` at this point are just number variables and nothing more; their names are to help us remember their purpose.

In line 18, we create a new list variable called `colour` containing each of these random values. Again, it's just a list with a convenient name containing three numbers of between 100 and 255 each. Finally, on line 19, the `return` command sends the list back to the line that called it (line 23).

Scope

Hold your horses – why does the variable `colour` appear twice? Surely that can't be right? It is right, because variables, by default, only exist inside the function that gives birth to them. This is what we call their *scope*. So, the variables within the `random_colour` function (`red`, `green`, `blue`, `colour`) can be accessed only by lines of code also inside that function. The `colour` variable defined at line 23 is not inside `random_colour`, so this part of the program can't "see" the one at line 18: this is why we must `return` it.

Having said that, if a function contains another function, then variables declared in the *parent* are accessible in the *child*. This is why `screen`, which is declared in the main code, can be used in `draw_circle`.

On the face of it, you might think it would make more sense to allow every part of a program to see and use variables from every other part, but there are two reasons why this isn't a good idea.

Firstly, each variable takes up memory and, since the variables within a function are there purely to help the function to perform its task, it would be wasteful to keep them "alive" once that task is complete. In fact, it might cause a program to run out of memory entirely.

Secondly, by keeping variables *local* to their function, we can reuse the variable name in other functions without causing a naming clash. This isn't just a matter of convenience: it also means that we can use reuse functions across lots of programs (including functions written by other people) without having to worry about accidentally duplicating variable names.

Occasionally, you do need to have access to a variable throughout the program. You can achieve this simply by using the `global` keyword in the line that originally defines the variable:

```
global my_var = 999
```

For the reasons given above you should only use global variables when absolutely necessary, and this is very rarely. There is usually a better way to do it that avoids the problems they create.

So, back to our program. The `random_colour` function generates a list with red, green and blue colour values and sends this list back to line 23. What happens next? On line 24, we call our other function `draw_circle`. This time the parameter is the colour we just received back from `random_colour`. On lines 9 and 10 we create random numbers between 1 and the width or height of the program window.

Most programming languages use a coordinate system, with the point at the top left-hand corner being 0,0. The *x* axis is left to right so, on line 9, we generate a horizontal position for our circle. The *y* axis is top to bottom, so line 10 generates a vertical coordinate. Line 11 generates a random number between 1 and 5, which will be the radius of the circle, and line 12 uses a function from the Pygame module to actually draw the circle on the screen.

When the interpreter reaches the end of line 12, it will see that there is no next line at the same tab level and go back to line 25 – there is no `return` statement this time because, well, there's nothing to return!

To make sure you understand, follow the order of the lines executed by the interpreter as it goes once through the loop from line 21:

21,22,23,14,15,16,17,18,19,24,8,9,10,11,12,25

Each of these iterations generates and displays one circle. Python repeats this until 100 have been generated, then drops down to line 27 to finish.

It's quite possible that, at this moment, your brain is smouldering – but don't worry! It all becomes natural very quickly, and this little program contains most of the key concepts you need to understand to become a coder. From here on in, it's a question of broadening your knowledge and applying it to more sophisticated (and more useful) apps.

Modules

Modules sound intimidating, but they're simply groups of functions that are saved in a separate text file and accessed by the interpreter as needed at runtime. In fact all Python files are modules, and the usual approach is to have one main module and one or more other modules with specific jobs. So, a word processor might – in addition to its main module – have modules called print.py, save.py and spellcheck.py.

Python comes with a range of standard modules – `random` and `math` are two that we've used already – and there's a huge selection of third-party modules, including `pygame`.

You might wonder why Python doesn't simply include all these functions into the main language, but it's a matter of efficiency: not all programs need random or maths functions, so the code is kept as lean as possible by only including the modules necessary to the particular task.

Python's built-in modules are available automatically. You simply use the `import` statement and they become usable. Third-party modules (including your

▶ **Focus On** ▶ **Colour** ████████████████████████

In Python, colours are made up by mixing red, green and blue, with each component colour assigned a value representing how strong it is. The possible values range from 0 to 255; in other words, there are 256 possibilities. This may seem odd – to a human it would make more sense if the range were set to 0-100, for example – but doing it this way makes complete sense to a computer.

Remember that, at their heart computers use binary notation. In binary, 255 is 11111111; or, put another way, 2^8. In other words, it's the largest number that can be written in eight bits or one byte of data. So, 0 represents none of that colour, and 255 represents 100% of it.

For our pygame circle, the mixed colour is written as a list of the three channels. Pure black would be [0,0,0] – in other words 0% of red, green and blue – and pure white is [255,255,255], with a mid-grey being [128,128,128]. Pure red would be [255,0,0], pure green [0,255,0] and a pure blue would be [0,0,255].

To get other colours, you simply mix the RGB channels. Magenta is [255,0,255] and yellow [255,255,0], whereas [128,64,0] makes a chocolate brown. Geany has a colour mixer built in, which you can use to work out the best values.

own) either have to be specially installed (as with **pygame**) or saved as .py files where the interpreter can find them. In practice, this usually means including them in the same folder as your code. Let's look at how we might *refactor* (improve) our colour circle program using modules. Here's the main module, which we've called snow.py:

```
1    import pygame, display
2    pygame.init()
3    clock = pygame.time.Clock() # Clock to limit speed
4    screen=display.setup()
5
6    for n in range(100):
7        clock.tick(45)
8        colour=display.random_colour(100,255)
9        display.draw_circle(colour,screen)
10       pygame.display.update()
11
12   raw_input("Press a key")
```

And here's a secondary module that we've called `display.py`:

```
1    import pygame, random
2    WIDTH=600; HEIGHT=600
3
4    def setup():
5        BLACK=(0,0,0)
6        screen = pygame.display.set_mode([WIDTH, HEIGHT])
7        screen.fill(BLACK)
8        return screen
9
10   def draw_circle(colour, screen):
11       x=random.randint(1,WIDTH)
12       y=random.randint(1,HEIGHT)
13       size=random.randint(1,5)
14       pygame.draw.circle(screen,colour,(x,y),size)
15
16   def random_colour(minimum, maximum):
17       red=random.randint(minimum,maximum)
18       green=random.randint(minimum,maximum)
19       blue=random.randint(minimum,maximum)
20       colour=[red,green,blue]
21       return colour
```

In a nutshell, we've exported all the functions to do with drawing to the screen to this new module called `display.py`. Doing this was simply a case of creating a new Python file in Geany and pasting the two existing functions into it. We've also added import statements for `pygame` and `random` to the top of this module, since they're needed by these functions, and we've moved the WIDTH and HEIGHT variable assignments to this module, too, since this is where they're used. The only major change we made is moving all the screen setup code into a function called setup.

Back in our original Python file (our `main` module), having moved the code across to `display.py`, we need to make a few other changes. Firstly, we need to import our new module on line 1 (note, we've removed the `random` import because it isn't needed for the code in this module). Secondly, we need to call the setup function in `display`.

There are a few things to notice here. Firstly, if we want to call a function in another module, we add the name of the module to the beginning so that Python knows where to find it. Secondly, if a function has no parameters, as here, we add empty brackets. Finally, note that the setup function returns a screen variable: this is because this variable is needed by the `draw_circle`. When we created our setup function, we put `screen` inside it. This means it's no longer accessible by `draw_circle`, so we must return it from `setup` to the main program; then, in line 9, we add it as a new parameter to our `draw_circle` code.

Whilst this might seem a bit of a palaver for very little gain, just take a look at `snow.py` in its new form. Remember, this is the main program. By removing much of the display code to another module, it's now much shorter and very clear. After all, we can understand what `draw_circle` and `random_colour` do from their names, so we don't need to see the code (unless there's a bug, in which case we know where to look!).

The more sophisticated your program, the more benefit you stand to gain from organising your code into modules. It's a good habit to get into thinking in modules right from the start.

A quick class in object-oriented programming

Many introductory books avoid explaining object-oriented development because it's seen as an advanced topic. But it's an essential part of modern-day programming, and something you'll need to understand if you're to do serious coding, let alone have a career in programming.

Fortunately, it's a pretty simple concept to get your head around – and it's very useful, especially for creating games, so we're going to tackle it head on. We'll leave some of the nitty-gritty to later chapters: for now the point is to understand what we're doing when we use object-oriented programming (OOP) techniques and why.

The basics
We introduced objects on page 35. Procedural programming is like writing code to directly control a puppet. Object-oriented programming is more like placing the code inside the puppet itself, so you can simply tell it what to do and it will go off and do it independently.

The code for an object is contained in a *class*. You can think of this as a blueprint. Each time a new object (sometimes called an *instance*) is needed, Python uses the class as its model for that object. In other words, if you needed lots of on-screen puppets, you could write just one class, then create a `for..in` loop to create hundreds at once.

One of the main benefits of OOP is *encapsulation*. This means that everything an object needs to know is contained within its own code. You could, in theory, take an object and use it in another program without having to change it at all.

In this way, objects are similar to modules, and they're made up of functions just as modules are (functions are often called *methods* when they're inside classes). Objects can sit within the main code, within modules, or in a file of their own. The more reusable they are, the more likely you'll want to store them separately.

Perhaps the most powerful feature of OOP is *inheritance*. Writing a single class for puppets is all very well, but marionettes come in many forms and the code for creating a Pinocchio would be different to that used for creating Mr Punch. Inheritance lets you define a generic class containing the code that applies to all puppets, and supplement it with child classes to define more specific cases.

So, let's say the generic class includes code for drawing a head, arms and legs. When we come to create the Pinocchio child class, we can simply write new code to add support for his extending nose. Mr Punch doesn't have standard puppet legs, so his child class might *override* the `draw_legs` function of the generic class with his own `draw_legs` function, whilst keeping all the rest of the code intact.

This approach means you, as a coder, only have to write the minimum code. It also becomes very easy to create new child classes, since most of the work is already done. And each change you make to the generic class is immediately inherited by all child classes, making bug fixing much simpler.

A simple class

Let's have a look at how we can revise our circle drawing program to use object-oriented principles. First we'll write the main module, below; then we'll add a module containing a class called `circle`, listed opposite:

```
1    import pygame, circle
2    pygame.init()
3    clock = pygame.time.Clock() # Clock to limit speed
4    WIDTH=600; HEIGHT=600
5    screen = pygame.display.set_mode([WIDTH, HEIGHT])
6    BLACK=(0,0,0)
7    screen.fill(BLACK)
8    circles=[]
9
10   for n in range(100):
11       clock.tick(45)
12       circles.append(circle.Circle(screen,WIDTH,HEIGHT))
13       pygame.display.update()
14
15   clock.tick(1)
16
17   for c in circles:
18       clock.tick(45)
19       c.clear_circle(screen)
20       pygame.display.update()
21
22   raw_input("Press a key")
```

```
1    import pygame, random
2
3    class Circle:
4        _minimum=100; _maximum=255
5        _colour=None
6        _properties=[]
7
8        def __init__(self,screen,width,height):
9            self.random_colour()
10           self.draw_circle(screen,width,height)
11
12       def draw_circle(self, screen, width, height):
13           x=random.randint(1,width)
14           y=random.randint(1,height)
15           size=random.randint(1,5)
16           self._properties=[x,y,size]
17           pygame.draw.circle(screen,self._colour,(x,y),size)
18
19       def random_colour(self):
20           red=random.randint(self._minimum,self._maximum)
21           green=random.randint(self._minimum,self._maximum)
22           blue=random.randint(self._minimum,self._maximum)
23           self._colour=[red,green,blue]
24
25       def clear_circle(self,screen):
26           pygame.draw.circle(screen,(0,0,0), ▶
     (self._properties[0], ▶
     self._properties[1]),self._properties[2])
```

The circle class completely replaces our display module. This in itself demonstrates object-oriented thinking: rather than creating a module that draws circles over the screen, we instruct each circle to draw itself. That's why we name the class this way.

You'll see immediately that two of the functions of the display module are present, largely unchanged, in our circle class. We begin with the keyword class, which is used to define the block containing all the code relating to that class. You can see that every line within the block is indented; again, this is how Python knows it belongs to the block.

Creating a class makes a special type of function available, which is always called __init__ (with two underscores either side of the name). This is short for "initialise" and, as you might imagine, is run when the object is first *instantiated* (created). In this case, the __init__ function automatically runs the two functions we created for the display module, so as soon as it's created our circle is drawn. This isn't always the case: the __init__ function is often used to set up the object for later use.

You may have spotted that the main difference in the code is the addition of the self keyword. This is critical to understanding how objects work. As you'd expect, self refers to the specific circle object being created at that moment. Remember the loop that runs 100 times in our main module? Each time it runs, it will create a new object, each of which has its own self. It's just as if you met 100 children: you might struggle to tell them apart, but each would themselves know who they were. So, each function has a self parameter that's used to refer to itself.

Finally, the other main change is that a new function called clear_circle has been created. Guess what this does? We've added a new variable to the object called _properties (note: it's a convention to use the underscore before the names of class variables, but it isn't compulsory) into which we save the *x* and *y* coordinates of this particular circle, along with its size.

Now go back to our main module. First, we replace display in the import statement with circle. You'll see that we've moved the initial setup code back

▶ Focus On ▶ Never do it twice

As a programmer, one of the most important attitudes to develop is a distaste for writing the same code twice. Whenever you find yourself repeating chunks of code, it should send a shiver down your spine: this is your warning that you should be finding a better way of doing it. For example, could you spin the code out into a function? This is marginally more hassle the first time you do it, but it pays dividends once you're able to use that function the second, third and fourth time.

In fact, most programming takes this organic form. You spot an inefficiency in your code and tidy it up by creating a function. Let's say, for example, that you find yourself asking the system to provide the current time repeatedly. This takes several lines of code because you want it returned in a specific way. You decide this would be better in a function so you create one.

Later, you find yourself doing a similar thing for the date or, perhaps, implementing a countdown timer. You create functions for each and then realise they could be organised together into a separate module called time_lib. This is great, but then you realise that you need to have multiple countdowns running at once – so you finally decide to take that particular function and turn it into a class.

here, because it doesn't make sense for it to be within the `circle` object. We also create an empty list called `circles`. Our main loop has become even simpler, and line 12 is the critical one. Just as with the `display` module, if we want to refer to a function within an imported class we must start with the name of the import – `circle` – followed by a full-stop and then by the name of the function.

In this case, because we're creating a new object, we simply refer to it. By convention, class names start with a capital letter, and our class name is `Circle` so that gets us to `circle.Circle`. This will run our `__init__` function, requiring three parameters of `screen`, `WIDTH` and `HEIGHT`. So now we have `circle.Circle(screen,WIDTH,HEIGHT)`. Finally, so that we can use our objects later, we load them into a list using the append method; this simply adds one to the end. We'll end up with a list that's 100 objects long.

So the effect of line 12 is to create a new object based on the `Circle` class (which results in a circle being drawn on the screen), and to add that object to a list. If we were just showing the circles, then the list wouldn't be needed but, as you can see in the second `for..in` loop, we also want to erase them.

Line 17, then, says "for every circle in the list"; line 18 sets the speed and then line 19 calls the `clear_circle` function in the class. So, it'll pull out each circle object, beginning with the first and, because each circle knows where it was painted on the screen and how big it was, we can use this self-awareness to paint a black circle on top, effectively erasing it.

The old-school way of doing this would have been to keep track of all of this within the main program. That's not as neat for a simple program such as this, and the more sophisticated a class is, the more useful it is to have objects look after themselves. It also makes it possible to reuse your code and objects elsewhere since they're fully self-contained.

Run the program (always run the main module, not the class) and you should see the random field of circles appear, pause for a moment, and then just as sedately disappear in reverse order.

This program has been an exercise rather than a functional application. For example, there's no user input at all. However, by adding input it could be turned into something more useful. Imagine if you painted circles across the whole screen and then paused the program. If you noted the position of the mouse pointer, you would be able to tell when it moved and respond by removing the circles using the code from line 17. What would you have? A simple screensaver – in fewer than 50 lines.

Again, don't worry if not all the principles of object-oriented programming have fully sunk in. The aim of this introduction is simply to start you thinking in an object-oriented way. You're now equipped with all the main concepts you need to build a career, or simply personal expertise, in programming. The rest of this book will help firm up what you've learned and show you how it works in practice as we create a working game.

Extending Python

We've already seen that Python has a number of built-in functions – for example, those that handle strings, lists and dictionaries – as well as a range of modules that are supplied with the language but must be *imported* before being used, such as those containing operations for random numbers and time. However, part of Python's great versatility comes from the huge library of free third-party modules out there. These range from very popular mainstream libraries, such as Pygame, to those aimed at niche uses, such as connecting a Raspberry Pi to a robot.

Let's take a quick look at some of the most important modules – especially those we're going to use in our game and project.

Pygame

Don't be fooled by the name: Pygame helps you develop games, but it can also do much more than that. Remember our clock widget, the first thing we coded to test our setup was working? We used Pygame to display the window and render the text in a nice form. Most of our examples so far have used Pygame, even though we haven't yet started coding a game. Pygame functions include:

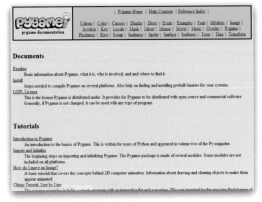

Pygame isn't just for creating games – download it from www.pygame.org

- **Display** Create windows, or allow games and projects to run full-screen;

- **Draw** Draw a whole range of *primitive* shapes such as rectangles, polygons, lines, ellipses, circles and arcs (and optionally fill them with colour);

- **Surface** Draw objects in memory, then paint them to the display in one go – essential for games with lots of graphics;

- **Font** Embed fonts into your project, so you can display them without relying on the end user having the same font installed on their system;

- **Image, Transform** A wide range of image manipulation functions that might be used to create specialised picture-processing applications;

- **Sprite** Create self-aware sprites with built-in collision detection, making complex games much simpler to create;

With the aid of Pygame it's possible to write professional-quality games in Python

• **Mixer, Music, Movie** Add sounds and videos to your projects;

• **Event** "Listen" for player action such as key presses or mouse movements.

Pygame is written mainly in C, so it gives good performance in games (remember that one of Python's strengths is its ability to use properly prepared C libraries). It's also available for a wide range of platforms: you can create games and apps for every mainstream desktop platform, and a few not-so-common ones!

Saving data

It's important to be able to save data between sessions, and load it back in as required – whether you want to allow users to save their position within a game, store records to a database or exchange information with a web server. Python offers a whole range of methods for achieving this, but the main ones – in order of increasing complexity – are: the File object, pickle and sqlite3.

File

The File object lets you create, save to, read from and delete text files. Anything you save is converted to text so, essentially, you're reading and writing strings. That doesn't mean you can't use File to handle sophisticated data, though. Let's take a very simple example. Type this listing into Geany and save it as file1.py:

```
1    first_name=raw_input('Type your first name...')
2    second_name=raw_input('Type your surname...')
3    savefile=open('data.dat','w')
4    savefile.write(first_name+'\n')
5    savefile.write(second_name+'\n')
6    savefile.close()
7    print('Saved')
8    first_name=None
9    second_name=None
10   openfile=open('data.dat','r')
11   name=openfile.read().split()
12   first_name=name[0]
13   second_name=name[1]
14   print first_name+" "+second_name
```

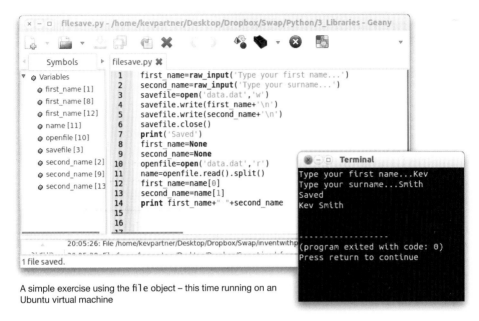

A simple exercise using the file object – this time running on an
Ubuntu virtual machine

Clearly, the first two lines ask the user to type in their first and second names. The interesting stuff begins on line 3, where we create a new variable using the file object's **open** method (remember, "functions" are called "methods" when inside objects). We pass in the name of the text file: this can be any name we choose as long as it's valid for our operating system (if the file doesn't exist, it will be created by Python at this point). The **'w'** parameter means that we want to write to the file; in other words, we want to save some data.

In line 4 we write the first name. By appending **'\n'** we add a new line. This is the file equivalent of pressing the Enter key – essentially we're using file to organise text by line, so by inserting a \n at this point the surname will appear separately a line below. You could also simply add a *delimiter* to each saved record – the pipe symbol "|", for example – but you must choose a character that you would never use within a record.

Having written the second name to the file, we then close it. This tells the operating system to save the file with its new contents.

We're now going to open it up again and read the contents back in. Lines 9 and 10 clear the name variables, so we can be sure we've read in the file and not simply kept what the user typed. On line 10 we create a new file object, using the same name, but this time with the parameter **'r'**, which reads in the contents of a file but leaves it unchanged. Since files only contain text, **openfile** is a string at the moment: this means we can use the **split()** function to take this text and create from it a list with each of the lines as a separate element.

For example, if the user's name was Jo Bloggs, printing *name* would result in:

['Jo','Bloggs']

To retrieve the first name we use name[0]; for the surname we use name[1]. Run the program and you'll see your name reappear in the terminal. There's an even better test, however: find the file data.dat (if you've used the same name) and open it in a text editor. You should see the names one per line. The file object is the workhorse of Python file input/output; it's pretty simple to use.

Pickle

The great benefit of pickle is that, unlike file, it can take any data form and save it to a file. It can also "unpickle" the data back to exactly its original form. In fact, pickle is specifically built to augment the built-in file object and make it more useful. Again, this is best understood through a short example, which we'll call pickleExample.py:

```
   import pickle
1  save_data={'username':'Joe Bloggs', ►
2  'score':9234,'max_level':5}
   save_file=open("savedata.dat",'wb')
3  pickle.dump(save_data,save_file)
4  save_file.close()
5  #zero variables, read file back in
6  progress_file=open("savedata.dat",'rb')
7  progress_data=pickle.load(progress_file)
8  print "Dear "+progress_data['username']+ ►
9  ", your data \n"+str(progress_data)
```

Note that we must begin with an import statement – pickle is part of the standard Python install but, because it isn't quite as basic an object as file, it must be explicitly added to the code. You don't have to install it, however, if you're using Windows, Mac or Linux (including Raspbian).

On line 2 we create a *dictionary* containing basic data, including the user's name, their current score and the furthest they've reached in our imaginary game. Next, we create a file object with the parameter 'wb', which stands for "write bytes". pickle uses its own storage format, so we need to specify that it's writing bytes of data, not text. This means the file it creates will look like gobbledygook if you open it in a text editor.

Line 4 uses the pickle.dump method to save the data – passing it the data itself (it could be any variable type, we're using a *dictionary*) and the file object. We then close the file.

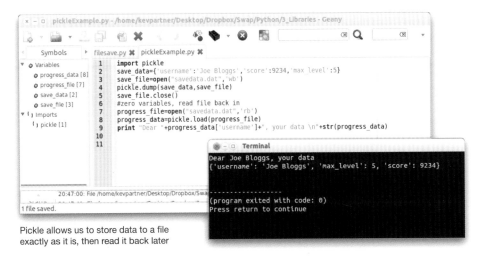

Pickle allows us to store data to a file
exactly as it is, then read it back later

In a real game, you'd probably want to read this data back in later or, indeed, in a later game session. The code from line 7 achieves this. We create a new `file` object, this time with the `'rb'` parameter because we're reading bytes back in. On line 8, we create a new variable and use it to receive the data from `pickle` using the `load` method. Line 9 prints it out.

`pickle` is a very powerful and widely used module. Its main advantage over the simpler `file` object is that you don't need to write code to *parse* (read and convert) the saved data when you want to retrieve it: `pickle` simply gives it back to you in the same format you used to save it. If you think about the amount of information you're likely to want to save in your game (a leaderboard, for example), you can appreciate how much simpler `pickle` makes this – not only saving time, but reducing the chances of bugs creeping in.

SQLite3

If you get into commercial programming then you'll encounter SQL (Structured Query Language – and no, it is *not* pronounced "Sequel") pretty quickly. This is a database system that's ideal for starting large amounts of structured data – such as for a customer database, or a football league manager game.

The main advantage of *relational databases* (the sort of databases SQL is most often used with) is that they make the retrieving of data lightning-quick. After all, if you have a large database of Conference League footballers and you want to list all players for sale, this needs to happen in the blink of an eye to avoid your game appearing slow.

SQLite is a halfway house between the ease of use and versatility of `pickle` and the full-fat power and complexity of, for example, MySQL (the database format used by a large percentage of websites). It's a cross-platform standard, represents data in a flat form similar in concept to card indexes. It isn't good at cross-indexing data but it's very good at simple retrieval – for example, it would make mincemeat of our "players for sale" query.

Python's SQLite3 module allows you to create, edit, read and write SQLite files and, if you intend to find work as a programmer, it's a good place to start learning about SQL whilst also being very useful. SQL itself is standard across its many forms so your experience of SQLite3 with Python would give you a head start when faced with learning any other mainstream database.

To do things with SQL databases, you write *queries* and then execute those queries using your chosen SQL engine. So, our Conference League player search might look something like this:

```
SELECT * FROM players WHERE league = 'conf' ▶
AND status = 'for sale'
```

It really is that straightforward – but since this isn't a book about SQL, we'll move along. The key point to bear in mind is that it's nothing to be frightened of. You can carry out most database functions with a small range of commonly used techniques.

Congratulations

So far in this book you've seen how to set up your Raspberry Pi and your coding environment. You've learnt how to think like a programmer. And you've had a whistle-stop tour of the basics of Python and object-oriented programming, so you now know the most useful variable types; how to create and use functions, modules and objects; and how to structure your code using decisions and loops. You've also learnt about the extra functionality Pygame adds, and explored the various ways to store and retrieve data using Python modules.

The best way to reinforce this knowledge and make sure it sticks is to put it into practice; so in the coming chapters we're going to cover, in great detail, the development of three very different projects. You've learned a lot so far, but don't worry if you don't remember everything we've covered – even the most experienced programmer considers Google to be their best friend. Programming is much more about technique and knowing which tool to use in a given situation than about remembering the specifics of how Python, or any other language, implements that tool.

Once you've completed the projects, you should have a very good idea of which situations call for a loop, which require a decision, and when it's best to spin out your functions into separate objects. This only comes through practise, so once again it's time to roll up your sleeves and get stuck in.

Chapter Four

Designing a game

In this section we're going to build on what we've learnt to design and create a simple game. By doing this, not only will we create an end product that will be fun to play, but we'll also explore many of the general programming skills you'll be able to transfer to future projects.

To get the most from this section, we strongly recommend that you type in the exercises as we go through. This way, you'll better understand what each line and statement does within the game. However, if you need to save time or check your work, the resources can also be downloaded from www.rpilab.net/code.

Fools rush in
However simple the game, you shouldn't just sit down at your computer and start coding right away – such an approach will result in nothing but chaos and frustration. You need to begin by thinking carefully about exactly how your game is going to work and, from that, generate a list of the tasks both you and your code will need to complete.

▶ **Focus On** ▶ **Specifications**

If you follow a career in programming, you'll quickly come across the concept of the "specification". This is a document that is created before programming starts and fully details what the application does, how it works and what it looks like. Different programming teams use different specifications and many now adopt a more rapid development approach called "agile", which minimises the up-front work and focuses more on smaller work units that evolve as the project progresses. For a simple game, our specification will be brief.

Genres of games

According to Wikipedia, there are 13 major genres of game, including action, role-playing, strategy, sports and puzzle. One way to come up with game ideas is to look through the genres and think about examples from each. Another option is to play plenty of games – on a phone, console or computer – and think about what you enjoy most. Don't bite off more than you can chew, though. A Space Invaders clone is certainly achievable by a new programmer, whereas a first person shooter inspired by *Call of Duty* probably isn't a realistic ambition – not as a first project, at least!

Pi Splat is a simple, fruit-based shoot-'em-up game

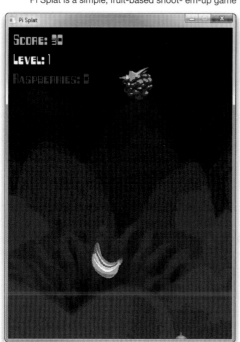

The concept

In this case, we're going to choose a simple shoot-'em-up called Pi Splat. We're using the Raspberry Pi as our inspiration so, naturally, our targets are going to be fruit. The concept can be summarised as:

We're being invaded! Several types of fruit fall from the top of the screen – but beware, most are poisonous. Use a mobile gun platform to destroy poisonous fruit, but allow raspberries through to reach the ground. When enough raspberries have landed, the planetary defences will be activated and the population will be saved.

Okay, it isn't exactly the most original concept but it's simple and fun – two excellent traits for our first game. Our next job is to decide on the rules for our game, and the victory conditions.

Rules

In real life there's nothing to stop you creating your own card game and making up the rules as you go along. However, the computer needs to know what to do in every conceivable situation. In this case, the game rules are simple.

1. Fruit appears randomly and drops vertically down the screen, disappearing if it reaches the bottom.

2. The gun turret can be moved left and right along the bottom of the screen. Pressing the Fire button launches a bullet up the screen.

3. If a bullet collides with a fruit, the fruit is destroyed.

4. If the destroyed fruit is not a raspberry, the player receives points.

5. If the destroyed fruit is a raspberry, the player loses points.

6. If a raspberry reaches the bottom of the screen, the player receives points.

7. If any other fruit reaches the bottom of the screen, the player loses points.

8. Once a set number of raspberries have reached the bottom, the level ends.

9. As levels pass, the speed of the falling fruit increases.

Victory condition

A game needs to have an aim. In games that have multiple levels, there is often one victory condition for the levels and a different, overall, aim for the game as a whole. For our game, the aim of each level is to collect the prescribed number of raspberries. The aim of the game as a whole is to clear 5 levels.

Now we have our rules and our victory condition, it's time to design the game, according to the principles of input, logic and output:

Input

The user needs to control the gun. This means we'll have to set up a way for the player to move it left and right, as well as firing. Keyboard control works best for a game of this sort, so we need to write code to specify which keys the player can use to control their gun turret and more code to "listen" for those key presses.

We'll also want the user to be able to save their progress so they can exit the game and resume later. So, when the game loads, it needs to check whether there's any progress data and, if so, read it as an input.

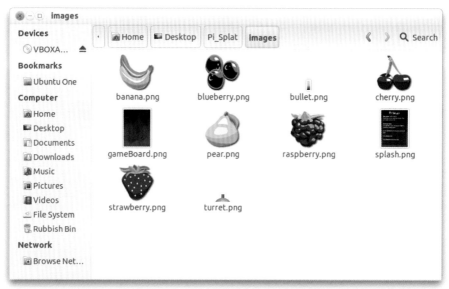

By looking at the game's output, we can generate a list of the graphics needed

Output

We'll need to create (or find) graphical images for each of the fruits that's going to appear in our game, and we'll need to write code to move them down the screen. To add a bit of visual interest, we'll also want to create an explosion effect for when the fruits are hit.

In addition, we'll need a turret graphic and bullets for the player – and this is also the right time to consider screen decorations for the background, over which we might display text for game instructions, score reports and so forth. In all we'll need the following graphics:

- Fruit (raspberry, cherry, strawberry, pear and banana)

- Player graphics (turret and bullets)

- Background graphic

- Splash screen

Sound is also a form of output, so we should also at this point consider whether we might want to include some in-game music and sound effects. Lastly, as mentioned opposite, we will also be saving the player's progress data to the hard disk – another form of output.

Logic

Lastly, our logic code will check whether bullets have collided with fruits, and update the score accordingly. It will also keep track of which level is being played, and when the game is over.

▶ Focus On ▶ Where to find graphics and sounds

You can download a huge quantity of graphical and audio resources from online libraries – but check the terms of use, especially if you intend to edit them. You can find free graphics at the Open Clip Art Library (`http://openclipart.org`), which you can normally edit and use as you wish. Fotolia (`http://en.fotolia.com`) provides top-quality graphics and photos for a small cost: for the best results, download the *vector* format of the image and edit it in a suitable program.

A good source of free sounds is `http://freesound.org`. You'll find everything here from music loops to special effects.

Creating the basic game

Now we've done our large-scale planning, you can finally open up your editor and start typing. We haven't yet worked out the fine details of how we're going to implement everything, but that's all right. Creating a game is a completely different process to building a real-world object such as a house. In that case you need a detailed blueprint before you dig the first hole. Programming is more like building a house out of Lego: you select from a toolset of pre-created blocks and build one part at a time, experimenting and amending along the way. It's an *iterative* and *organic* process, in which you focus on the building blocks of the program – writing, testing and editing code to create each function, module and class – before bringing them together to make the final product.

Getting started

We'll begin by creating a simple template for our game, then fill in the code to get the game working. To create the template, we need to think about how our code will be organised in terms of graphics, sounds and Python files – and we do this using the familiar structure of input, logic and output from the previous chapter.

Broadly speaking, you should expect to create a class for each of the game's visible objects. You could add the code for each of these classes in the main Python file, but it makes more sense to have each in its own file: this is clearer and easier to understand, and removes clutter from the main program code.

▶ **Focus On** ▶ Using external resources

You can find the code, images and other resources for this game at www. rpilab.net/code. You'll find specific information about Pygame functions at www.pygame.org/docs and documentation for Python 2.7 is at http:// docs.python.org/2/index.html.

Important: we're not going to go into detail about every single command used in this code. You've met much of it earlier in this book, and where a command or function is new we'll explain what it does; but we expect you to use the documentation for Python and Pygame to learn the detail. Not only does this help us make progress, it encourages a key skill every modern day programmer needs: the ability to use documentation.

You'll also notice our code doesn't include many programming comments (explanatory text following the # symbol). This is to keep our listings clean and short. The downloadable code (which you should look through after completing the chapter) is heavily documented.

1. Main.py
Create a folder to contain your Python game. Now, in Geany, create and save a file called main.py. Type in the code in listing 1 (overleaf) and save it.

2. Classes
Create Python files named bullet.py, fruit.py, turret.py and game.py. The first three are straight out of our design document and represent visible objects. The game class is there to hold information about the game as a whole. For example, it can keep track of the player's score and level number, and can be conveniently reused across multiple projects

Add the following text to the top of each of the class files:

```
class Bullet():
    def __init__(self):
        pass
```

...replacing Bullet with the name of each class. The pass command is simply a placeholder – it doesn't do anything, but if we didn't provide it Python would report an error since it isn't valid to define a completely empty function.

3. Images
Finally, in your project folder, create a subfolder called "images" and copy all the game's graphic files into it, so they're in a convenient place for us to access later.

▶ Focus On ▶ Picture and sound formats

The images used in this game are saved in PNG (Portable Network Graphics) format. This is because PNGs can have transparent backgrounds; if you used the popular JPEG format, for example, you'd see a white edge around each of the fruits. When developing games for the Raspberry Pi, you need to choose the most efficient format for each graphic, and for those with transparent backgrounds the 8-bit PNG format with alpha transparency works well.

As you'll remember, an 8-bit image can include only a maximum of 256 colours (a 32-bit PNG can contain millions of colours), so this also gives the Pi less work to do when it's painting each screen. For most purposes, this is the format to use.

When it comes to sound, WAV is a good format for short noises. Although the file size is larger than MP3, files in this format aren't compressed, so your computer doesn't have to do any unnecessary work to play them. For longer sounds that are loaded once at the start of the game – background music, for example – MP3 is a better choice so as not to waste valuable disk space and memory.

Main.py – the "boilerplate" of our program

```
1    import math,random,pygame,sys
2    from fruit import *; from game import *; ▶
     from turret import *; from bullet import *
3
4    ##TOP LEVEL CONSTANTS
5    FPS = 30
6    WINDOWWIDTH=480; WINDOWHEIGHT=640
7    GAMETITLE="Pi Splat"
8    WHITE=[255,255,255]; RED=[255,0,0]; GREEN=[0,255,0];
9    BLUE=[0,0,255]; BLACK=[0,0,0]
10
11   def main():
12       #set up initial display
13       pygame.init()
14       clock=pygame.time.Clock()
15       surface=pygame.display.set_mode ▶
         ([WINDOWWIDTH,WINDOWHEIGHT])
16       pygame.display.set_caption(GAMETITLE)
17
```

```
18        #MAIN GAME LOOP
19        game_over=False
20
21        while game_over==False:
22            for event in pygame.event.get():
23                if event.type==pygame.KEYDOWN:
24                    if event.key==pygame.K_ESCAPE:
25                        game_over=True
26            print pygame.time.get_ticks()
27            pygame.display.update()
28            clock.tick(FPS)
29
30    if __name__ == '__main__':
31        main()
```

The initial 31 lines of our program comprise the "boilerplate", or standard structure, which hardly varies from game to game. Line 2 imports our classes. We then set a series of *constants*: variables whose values will not change during the game. Unlike many other languages, Python doesn't have a separate type for constants, so we name them using capital letters so we can identify them later.

On line 11 we set up a function called main, which is where our program will begin. Lines 13-16 use pygame functions to draw the initial window for the game. Lines 21 to 28 constitute the *main loop*: this is the code used to draw the screen many times per second as the game is being played.

We set up a variable called game_over in line 19 and give it the value False. We then start a while loop that will keep repeating until game_over becomes True. The for loop at line 22 asks Pygame if any *events* have taken place. In this case, we're interested in keyboard events so, in line 23, we cycle through all the events in the queue and, if a key has been pressed, we then ask if that key was "Esc". If it was, we set game_over to True, causing the game to exit.

Line 27 updates the display (we haven't yet added anything visual, but will do soon) and line 28 tells Pygame to make sure the loop doesn't cycle more quickly than 30 times per second. Finally, lines 30 and 31 are used to make sure that the main function will be accessed only if this was the file open in Geany when we clicked the cog button. In other words, if we accidentally imported this module into another, *main* would not be called.

Once you've entered and checked all this code, click the cog icon (or press F5). You should see a series of numbers running down the terminal window: these are generated by line 25 and are simply the number of milliseconds since the program started, proving that you've typed everything correctly and are ready to move on. If you see any error messages in the terminal window, you need to correct them before continuing.

Let there be fruit

Now it's time to make the fruit appear and drop down the screen. We'll start by setting up the fruit object. Open up `fruit.py` in Geany and type in this code:

```
1    import pygame, random
2    class Fruit(pygame.sprite.Sprite):
3
4        def __init__(self,WINDOWWIDTH):
5            pygame.sprite.Sprite.__init__(self)
6            self._species=random.choice(["raspberry", ▶
     "strawberry", "cherry","pear","banana"])
7            self.image=pygame.image.load("images/"+ ▶
     self._species+".png")
8            self.rect=self.image.get_rect()
9            self.rect.y=0-self.rect.height
10           self.rect.x=(random.randint(self.rect. ▶
     width/2,(WINDOWWIDTH-self.rect.width)))
11
12       def update_position(self,speed,WINDOWHEIGHT,game):
13           if self.rect.y<(WINDOWHEIGHT):
14               self.rect.y+=speed*5
15           else:
16               if self._species=="raspberry":
17                   game.update_score(50)
18                   game.update_raspberries_saved()
19               else:
20                   game.update_score(-10)
21               self.kill()
22
23       def shot(self,game):
24           if self._species=="raspberry":
25               game.update_score(-50)
26           else:
27               game.update_score(10)
28           self.kill()
```

We begin by importing the pygame library and the random module. Take a look at line 2 – you can see that we've added `pygame.sprite.Sprite` to the class definition. This is an example of class inheritance in action: this line tells Python to create a new object based on Pygame's `Sprite` class, so Python will assume that this object *is* a sprite in all its behaviours and properties – except where we explicitly specify otherwise. A sprite is a specialised object that's based on an image and which can be easily moved around the screen. It contains all the functions needed to handle the visual side of our fruit.

The `__init__` function is run when the main program creates a new *instance* of the Fruit class. In other words, when we want a new fruit to appear and fall down the screen. In line 6 we create a *property* of the sprite that we've named `_species`. In reality it's just a variable like any other, but the convention is to call variables that are inside objects "properties".

The `self` keyword in front of a variable name tells the object that this variable is part of its unique identity and should be remembered. So every Fruit instance will remember which species it was set to for as long as it's alive; this is a very useful feature of objects, as we'll see.

In line 7, we use Pygame's `image` functions to load a picture into the sprite. The next line makes sure that the size of the sprite matches the size of the image just loaded. Line 9 sets the *y* (vertical) position to zero minus the height of the image. So if the picture was 50 pixels tall, the top-left corner of the fruit will be drawn at -50, so it's just off the top of the screen.

Line 10 looks a little bit more complicated, but it simply specifies a random horizontal (*x*) position for the fruit. The `random.randint` function takes two parameters, to set the range between which you want it to generate a number. Our first parameter – the lower bound – is :

```
self.rect.width/2
```

In other words, we want the lowest possible horizontal value to be half the width of the image from the left. This ensures the fruit will never be drawn either wholly or partially off the left edge of the screen. The second parameter, specifying the upper bound, is:

```
WINDOWWIDTH-self.rect.width
```

In this case, the maximum right-hand position will be the width of the window minus the width of the image. So with a `WINDOWWIDTH` of 480 pixels and a fruit width of, say, 72 pixels, we'd be asking `random.randint` to provide a random number between 36 (72/2) and 408 (480-72). That number would be used to position the fruit: each one in a different horizontal location.

The `__init__` function, then, sets things up, but we need to add more functions to make things happen. These functions will vary depending on the purpose of the class, and in this case the most obvious attribute of our fruit is that it moves down the screen, so we'll begin with a function called `update_position`. Unlike `__init__`, this function will only run when it's called (in this case, by the main program).

The function definition in line 12 includes four parameters that must be passed to it. `self` is part of all class definitions, but the others are our own variables. `WINDOWHEIGHT` is self-explanatory, `game` is the game object (we haven't created it yet) and `speed` is a parameter we'll set in `main.py` shortly.

The function is pretty simple. On line 13 we check to see if the vertical position of the fruit is still less than the height of the window (if it isn't, then the fruit must have dropped off the bottom). If it is, then in line 14 we increase its *y* position by an amount related to the speed.

If the fruit *has* dropped out of the window then Python will execute the code after the `else` in line 15. In this case, the code is another `if` statement: it's very important to understand that the code between lines 16 and 21 will *only* be executed if line 13 is `false`.

So, on line 16 we check to see if the current fruit is a raspberry. Remember that the point of the game is to allow raspberries to reach the bottom of the screen, so, in that case, we are going to increase the score and increment the number of raspberries saved so far (the game ends when this number gets to ten). Note that we haven't actually added any code to the game object yet, but we now know which functions to create.

Line 19 translates as "if the fruit is not on-screen (because it's reached the bottom) and it's not a raspberry then execute the next line". In this case, line 20 decreases the score because the player has allowed one of the other fruits to reach the bottom.

Finally, line 21 deletes the object. Look closely at the indentation to make sure you understand the circumstances under which this line will be executed: the `self.kill` function is *not* inside the `if` structure starting on line 16, so if the object has fallen off the bottom of the screen it will be "killed" whichever fruit

▶ **Focus On** ▶ **Why use variables for constants?**

You'll have noticed that once we've set the value of `WINDOWWIDTH` in `main.py`, it stays the same throughout our game – that's why we call it a constant and why, conventionally, we write it all in capital letters. So why do we bother with it? Why don't we just specify the value 480 directly when we need to refer to the width of the window?

We do it this way for two reasons. Firstly, because this allows you to create a new game – with a different width – by doing nothing more than changing a value once at the start of the program, rather than having to find and alter every occurrence of 480. The second reason is that it makes reading your code much simpler. By using `WINDOWWIDTH` rather than 480 in a calculation, you know exactly what that number represents.

type it represents. Although the fruit is no longer visible, it makes sense to clear it and stop it updating: otherwise it will continue to fall, even though we can't see it, pointlessly wasting computing power and memory.

Finally, since the object of the game is to shoot fruit (except raspberries), we add a function called shot. A quick look over the code should be ample for you to see what it does.

Setting up the game

```
1    class Game():
2        def __init__(self):
3            self._score=0
4            self._raspberries_saved=0
5
6        def update_score(self,amount):
7            self._score+=amount
8
9        def get_score(self):
10           return self._score
11
12       def update_raspberries_saved(self):
13           self._raspberries_saved+=1
14
15       def get_raspberries_saved(self):
16           return self._raspberries_saved
```

Having written our Fruit class, we now know what we need (initially, at least) to include in our Game class (save it as game.py). Remember that this is a different sort of class to Fruit: it doesn't relate to a visible object on-screen. It's simply a convenient wrapper for code and variables that relate to the game as a whole.

The class definition doesn't contain anything between the brackets because we're not basing Game on a pre-existing class. The __init__ function initialises two variables – the score and the number of raspberries we've saved – so we can use them later. update_score takes the amount sent to it and adds that to the running score (see line 17 of fruit.py to see this function called). get_score, on the other hand, uses the return keyword to send back the score. So, we could write a line of code like this to print the current score to the terminal:

```
print game.get_score
```

The final two functions fulfil the same purpose for the raspberries_saved variable, so our program can easily check this value too.

Updating Main.py

It's time to fill out the "boilerplate" code we created earlier, to accommodate the additional features needed to work with our fruit sprites. Update your `main.py` module as follows:

```
1    import math,random,pygame,sys
2    from fruit import *; from game import *; ▶
     from turret import *; from bullet import *
3
4    ##TOP LEVEL CONSTANTS
5    FPS = 30
6    WINDOWWIDTH=480; WINDOWHEIGHT=640
7    GAMETITLE="Pi Splat"
8    WHITE=[255,255,255]; RED=[255,0,0]; GREEN=[0,255,0]; ▶
     BLUE=[0,0,255]; BLACK=[0,0,0]
9    SPEED=0.5
10
11   def main():
12     game=Game()
13
14     #set up initial display
15     pygame.init()
16     clock=pygame.time.Clock()
17     surface=pygame.display.set_mode([WINDOWWIDTH,WINDOWHEIGHT])
18     pygame.display.set_caption(GAMETITLE)
19
20     #MAIN GAME LOOP
21     game_over=False
22     live_fruit_sprites=pygame.sprite.Group()
23     ticktock=1
24     while game_over==False:
25       for event in pygame.event.get():
26         if event.type==pygame.KEYDOWN:
27           if event.key==pygame.K_ESCAPE:
28             game_over=True
29
30       if ticktock % (FPS/SPEED)==1:
31         if len(live_fruit_sprites)<10:
32           live_fruit_sprites.add((Fruit(WINDOWWIDTH)))
33
34       surface.fill(BLACK)
```

```
35          for sprite in live_fruit_sprites:
36              sprite.update_position(SPEED,WINDOWHEIGHT,game)
37
38          live_fruit_sprites.draw(surface)
39
40          pygame.display.update()
41
42          ticktock+=1
43
44          clock.tick(FPS)
45
46  if __name__ == '__main__':
47      main()
```

You'll see we've made quite a few changes. We've added a new constant called SPEED at line 9; and at line 22 we create a sprite group. This is essentially a list of all the fruit sprites so we can easily handle them later.

The if statement beginning at line 31 checks if there are fewer than ten fruits on the screen, and if so creates a new fruit object and adds it to the sprite group. You'll notice we created a variable called ticktock on line 23, and we use it on line 30. This is needed because the main loop (beginning at line 24) runs at 30 frames per second (see line 44). Without the code at line 30, all the fruits would be added almost instantly rather than spread out.

At line 42, ticktock increments each loop, so it'll be worth 30 after one second, 60 after two seconds and so on. Line 30 says that if you divide ticktock by the number of frames per second (30 in this case), divided by the speed variable (0.5 at the moment), and get a remainder of 1 (that's what the % or *modulus* means), run line 31 and add a fruit if there are fewer than ten. It's a bit of a brain-melter, but if you think it through, you'll see that

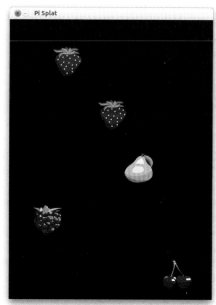

Run the code and you should now see fruit falling randomly down the window

there will be a remainder of 1 when `ticktock` is worth 61, 121, 181 and so forth. The effect, then, is to run line 32 every two seconds or so – which is exactly what we want. Alternatively, we could use Python's time functions, but doing it this way keeps things in sync if the computer struggles to keep up for any reason.

Line 34 fills the window with black (you'll be able to see what happens if you don't do this in a moment). Line 35 cycles through every fruit (if there are any) and, in line 36, runs the Fruit class's `update_position` function we just created, moving each one down the screen or deleting it. Finally, we run Pygame's `draw` function, which will paint every fruit to the screen in one go.

Give it a try. Make sure `main.py` is in your Geany window and press F5 or click the cog. You should see fruit appear at the top and move smoothly down the window. Close the terminal to stop the program and add a hash symbol (#) to the start of line 34; this "comments out" the line so that Python ignores it. Press F5 and you should see a very different result.

Shooting fruit

We're only a few steps away from having a working game, so let's press on and add the missing sections of code. We'll start with the gun turret: enter the code below and save it as `turret.py`:

```
1   import pygame
2   class Turret(pygame.sprite.Sprite):
3       def __init__(self,WINDOWWIDTH,WINDOWHEIGHT):
4           pygame.sprite.Sprite.__init__(self)
5           self.image=pygame.image.load("images/turret.png")
6           self.rect = self.image.get_rect()
7           self.rect.x = (WINDOWWIDTH-self.rect.width)/2
8           self.rect.y =WINDOWHEIGHT-self.rect.height
9
10      def update_position(self,direction,WINDOWWIDTH):
11          if direction=="left" and self.rect.x>10:
12              self.rect.x-=10
13          elif direction=="right" and ►
        self.rect.x<(WINDOWWIDTH-10):
14              self.rect.x+=10
15
16      def get_gun_position(self):
17          position={}
18          position["x"]=self.rect.x+(self.rect.width/2)
19          position["y"]=self.rect.y-(self.rect.height/2)
20          return position
```

This class is similar to the Fruit class, with lines 7 and 8 positioning the turret graphic at the centre of the screen's bottom edge. At line 10 we set up the update_position method, which takes the direction and the width of the window as parameters and either deducts from the turret's horizontal (*x*) position to send the graphic left, or adds to it to send it right. See if you can work out how the code prevents the turret from disappearing off the side of the screen.

Finally, starting at line 16, we add a function to send back the position of the gun in the centre of the turret, so we can make bullets appear like they're emerging from the gun. Here's the code for the last class, bullet.py:

```
1    import pygame
2    class Bullet(pygame.sprite.Sprite):
3        def __init__(self,position):
4            pygame.sprite.Sprite.__init__(self)
5            self.image=pygame.image.load("images/bullet.png")
6            self.rect = self.image.get_rect()
7            self.rect.x=position["x"]
8            self.rect.y=position["y"]
9
10       def update_position(self):
11
12           if self.rect.y>=-self.rect.height:
13               self.rect.y-=5
14           else:
15               self.kill()
```

In the __init__ function, we send the gun position from Turret. The function update_position is very simple; since bullets go *up* the screen, their *y* value gets smaller as they move. Once they go off the top, we destroy the sprite.

Main.py – the first fully working version

Now we've set up the code to handle our turret and bullets, we simply need to make a few last changes to main.py to tie it all together and finish the first version of the game. We've marked the changes in red, below:

```
1    import math,random,pygame,sys
2    from fruit import *; from game import *; ▶
3    from turret import *; from bullet import *
4
5    ##TOP LEVEL CONSTANTS
6    FPS = 30
```

```
7    WINDOWWIDTH=480; WINDOWHEIGHT=640
8    GAMETITLE="Pi Splat"
9    WHITE=[255,255,255]; RED=[255,0,0]; GREEN=[0,255,0]; ▶
     BLUE=[0,0,255]; BLACK=[0,0,0]
10   SPEED=0.5
11
12   def main():
13       game=Game()
14
15       #set up initial display
16       pygame.init()
17       pygame.key.set_repeat(1, 75)
18       scoreFont=pygame.font.Font("256BYTES.TTF",32)
19       clock=pygame.time.Clock()
20       surface=pygame.display.set_mode([WINDOWWIDTH,WINDOWHEIGHT])
21       pygame.display.set_caption(GAMETITLE)
22
23       #MAIN GAME LOOP
24       game_over=False
25       live_fruit_sprites=pygame.sprite.Group()
26       bullet_sprites=pygame.sprite.Group()
27       other_sprites=pygame.sprite.Group()
28       turret=Turret(WINDOWWIDTH,WINDOWHEIGHT)
29       other_sprites.add(turret)
30       ticktock=1
31
32       while game_over==False:
33           for event in pygame.event.get():
34               if event.type==pygame.KEYDOWN:
35                   if event.key==pygame.K_ESCAPE:
36                       game_over=True
37                   elif event.key==pygame.K_LEFT:
38                       turret.update_position("left",WINDOWWIDTH)
39                   elif event.key==pygame.K_RIGHT:
40                       turret.update_position("right",WINDOWWIDTH)
41                   elif event.key==pygame.K_SPACE:
42                       bullet=Bullet(turret.get_gun_position())
43                       bullet_sprites.add(bullet)
44
45           if ticktock % (FPS/SPEED)==1:
46               if len(live_fruit_sprites)<10:
47                   live_fruit_sprites.add((Fruit(WINDOWWIDTH)))
```

```
48
49          for sprite in bullet_sprites:
50              sprite.update_position()
51
52          collisions=pygame.sprite.groupcollide(live_fruit_ ▶
      sprites,bullet_sprites,False,True)
53
54          if collisions:
55              for fruit in collisions:
56                  fruit.shot(game)
57
58          surface.fill(BLACK)
59          bullet_sprites.draw(surface)
60          other_sprites.draw(surface)
61
62          for sprite in live_fruit_sprites:
63              sprite.update_position(SPEED,WINDOWHEIGHT,game)
64
65          live_fruit_sprites.draw(surface)
66
67          scoreText=scoreFont.render('Score: '+str(game.get_ ▶
      score()),True,GREEN)
68          surface.blit(scoreText,(10,10))
69          pygame.display.update()
70
71          ticktock+=1
72          if game.get_raspberries_saved()>=10:
73              game_over=True
74
75          clock.tick(FPS)
76
77      #handle end of game
78      surface.fill(BLACK)
79      scoreText=scoreFont.render('Game over. Score: '▶
      +str(game.get_score()),True,GREEN)
80      surface.blit(scoreText,(10,200))
81      pygame.display.update()
82
83      raw_input("press any key")
84
85  if __name__ == '__main__':
86      main()
```

Line 17 calls a `Pygame` function that limits the repeat interval on a keypress to 75 milliseconds, so the player can hold down the spacebar and rapidly fire a stream of bullets. Line 18 imports a custom font (`www.1001freefonts.com` is a good place to find them) that we'll use to display the score. In lines 26 to 29, we create two new sprite groups: one to hold the bullets, and a second catch-all group for any other sprites we're adding.

Lines 37 to 40 respond to the left and right arrow keys, updating the turret's position using the code we just added to `turret.py`. Lines 41 to 43 create a new bullet when the spacebar is pressed and add the bullet to the group. Lines 49 and 50 cycle through all the bullets currently visible and trigger the `update_position` function for each in turn.

Line 52 is a little bit of Pygame magic. This one line checks whether *any* bullet has collided with *any* fruit. If one has, Pygame generates a *list* of those fruits that have collided. All we have to do is pass in the two sprite groups we want to check (hence our maintaining separate groups for bullets and fruit), along with parameters indicating whether Pygame should kill colliding sprites. For the fruit, we send a `False` parameter because we want to update the score before killing them manually. For the bullets, it's fine for Pygame to kill them.

In lines 54 to 56, we iterate through any collisions and run the `shot` function of the fruit the bullet has hit. Lines 59 and 60 draw the new groups to the screen.

On line 67 we use Pygame's `font.render` to create a picture that displays the score in green with a transparent background. Line 68 paints the score onto the screen using the `blit` function. You must use this function to draw objects onto the screen if you're not using sprites, otherwise they won't appear.

Lines 72 and 73 set up a simple `if` statement that breaks out of the main game loop once we've saved 10 raspberries. Finally, the code from lines 78 to 83 clears the screen, draws the final score and waits for the user to press a key.

Once your code matches our listings, save and press F5 to play the game. Whilst it's certainly basic, you now have a fully working, playable, arcade game in fewer than 200 lines of code. Not bad!

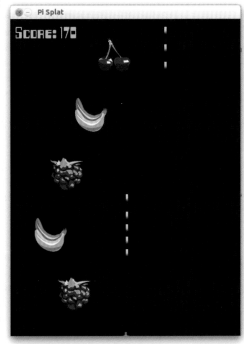

Our code allows the player to hold down the spacebar to loose off a hail of bullets

Completing the game

To add a bit of depth to Pi Splat, we might add levels that become progressively harder. While we're at it, we should also implement the additional input and output functions we planned at the start: adding a splash/instructions screen at the start of the game, and giving the player the ability to save and restore the player's progress. We'll also smooth out a few rough edges to give the game a more professional polish.

Rather than typing in all the code that follows, we recommend you download the complete version of the game from www.rpilab.net/code, load it into Geany and follow the discussion.

The finished code

Most of the remaining work takes place in main.py. This makes sense, as adding levels doesn't affect the way individual objects such as fruits or bullets behave.

On line 1, we add two new modules: pickle and os. Both are needed so that we can save the user's progress. We remove the SCORE constant and replace it with NUMBER_OF_LEVELS, which we're setting to five. You can change the number of levels in your version of the game by altering this number.

Starting at line 23, we've added some code to create a splash screen. This has been created as a single graphic. It might have been more flexible to add the text at runtime, but a static image is fine for a simple game such as this.

```
1    import math,random,pygame,sys,pickle,os
2    from fruit import *; from game import *; ▶
     from turret import *; from bullet import *
3
4    ##TOP LEVEL CONSTANTS
5    FPS = 30
6    WINDOWWIDTH=480; WINDOWHEIGHT=640
7    GAMETITLE="Pi Splat"
8    WHITE=[255,255,255]; RED=[255,0,0]; GREEN=[0,255,0]; ▶
     BLUE=[0,0,255]; BLACK=[0,0,0]
9    NUMBER_OF_LEVELS=5
10
11   def main():
12       game=Game()
```

```
13
14      #INITIAL SETUP
15      pygame.init()
16      pygame.key.set_repeat(1, 75)
17      pygame.mouse.set_visible(False)
18      displayFont=pygame.font.Font("256BYTES.TTF",28)
19      clock=pygame.time.Clock()
20      surface=pygame.display.set_mode([WINDOWWIDTH, ►
    WINDOWHEIGHT])
21      pygame.display.set_caption(GAMETITLE)
22
23      #SPLASH SCREEN
24      splash=pygame.image.load("images/splash.png")
25      surface.blit(splash,(0,0))
26      pygame.display.update()
27      game_over=False
28      start_game=False
29
30      while start_game==False:
31          for event in pygame.event.get():
32              if event.type==pygame.KEYDOWN:
33                  if event.key==pygame.K_ESCAPE:
34                      game_over=True
35                  elif event.key==pygame.K_RETURN or ►
    event.key==pygame.K_KP_ENTER:
36                      resume=False
37                      start_game=True
38                  elif event.key==pygame.K_LSHIFT or ►
    event.key==pygame.K_RSHIFT:
39                      resume=True
40                      start_game=True
41
42      if resume==True: #if they want to pick up a saved game
43          if os.path.exists("savedata.dat")==True:
44              game.load_game()
```

At line 24, we load the splash screen and blit it to the surface on line 25, before refreshing the screen so it becomes visible. We've moved the game_over variable to this point so the user can exit even when a game isn't underway.

Lines 30 to 40 wait for the user to press a key, and respond when he or she does. The instructions tell them to press Enter to start a new game or Shift to resume an existing one. Since there are two physical Enter keys (the one under

Backspace and the one alongside the numeric keypad), we have to handle this in line 35. Similarly, there are two Shift keys: line 38 captures this and sets the resume variable to True.

On line 42, we check to see if they chose to continue an existing game, but we first need to check if a save file already exists (there won't be one if it's the first time they've played the game). This is achieved through the os ("operating system") module function. On line 44, we run a yet-to-be-created function of the game object. The code continues:

```
45
46       #MAIN GAME LOOP
47       while game.get_level()<=NUMBER_OF_LEVELS and ▶
    game_over==False:
48
49           #SHOW LEVEL NUMBER
50           surface.fill(BLACK)
51           levelText=displayFont.render('Level: '▶
    +str(game.get_level()),True,GREEN)
52           surface.blit(levelText,(150,300))
53           pygame.display.update()
54           pygame.time.wait(1500)
55
56           #SET UP VARIABLES FOR LEVEL
57           game.save_game()
58           live_fruit_sprites=pygame.sprite.Group()
59           game._raspberries_saved=0
60           bullet_sprites=pygame.sprite.Group()
61           other_sprites=pygame.sprite.Group()
62           turret=Turret(WINDOWWIDTH,WINDOWHEIGHT)
63           other_sprites.add(turret)
64           ticktock=1
65           level_over=False
```

We've added a new loop that runs while the current level is less than or equal to the total number of levels and the user hasn't pressed Escape. Before each level begins, we want to display a text message, so on lines 50 to 54 we erase the splash screen (by filling it with black) and set up a font. We've changed the name of this variable from scoreFont because it now has a more general use.

We then use Pygame's time.wait() function to pause for 1.5 seconds, after which we start the code for each level (remember, the code after line 47 runs each time a new level is started). On line 57 we run another function of game – one we haven't yet written – to save progress. Why save it now? Because we want the user to come back at the start of the level they were playing when they exited, so we save the state before it begins. The only other changes to this block of code are that we zero the variable game._raspberries_saved before the level starts and we create a new variable level_over.

```
66
67              #PLAY INDIVIDUAL LEVEL
68              while level_over==False and game_over==False:
69                  for event in pygame.event.get():
70                      if event.type==pygame.KEYDOWN:
71                          if event.key==pygame.K_ESCAPE:
72                              game_over=True
73                          elif event.key==pygame.K_LEFT:
74                              turret.update_position("left", ▸
       WINDOWWIDTH,game.get_level())
75                          elif event.key==pygame.K_RIGHT:
76                              turret.update_position("right", ▸
       WINDOWWIDTH,game.get_level())
77                          elif event.key==pygame.K_SPACE:
78                              bullet=Bullet(turret.get_gun_position())
79                              bullet_sprites.add(bullet)
80
81                  if ticktock >=120:
82                      ticktock=0
83                      if len(live_fruit_sprites)<10:
84                          live_fruit_sprites.add((Fruit(WINDOWWIDTH)))
85
86                  for sprite in bullet_sprites:
87                      sprite.update_position()
88
89                  collisions=pygame.sprite.groupcollide ▸
       (live_fruit_sprites,bullet_sprites,False,True)
90
91                  if collisions: #if there are any
92                      for fruit in collisions:
93                          fruit.shot(game)
94
95                  background=pygame.image.load ▸
97       ("images/gameBoard.png")
97                      surface.blit(background,(0,0))
98                      bullet_sprites.draw(surface)
99                      other_sprites.draw(surface)
```

```
100             for sprite in live_fruit_sprites:
101                 sprite.update_position ▶
        (game.get_level(),WINDOWHEIGHT,game)
102                 live_fruit_sprites.draw(surface)
103
104             scoreText=displayFont.render ▶
        ('Score: '+str(game.get_score()),True,GREEN)
105             levelText=displayFont.render ▶
        ('Level: '+str(game.get_level()),True, WHITE)
106             raspberriesText=displayFont.render ▶
        ('Raspberries: '+str(game.get_raspberries_saved()),True,RED)
107             surface.blit(scoreText,(10,10))
108             surface.blit(levelText,(10,50))
109             surface.blit(raspberriesText,(10,90))
110             pygame.display.update()
111             ticktock+=game.get_level()
112
113             if game.get_raspberries_saved()>=10:
114                 game.update_level(1)
115                 level_over=True
116             clock.tick(FPS)
```

You'll notice that all of this code has been indented by an additional tab (do this in Geany by highlighting the lines you want to indent and pressing Tab once). If you think this through you'll see that we've done this because, at the end of each level, we want to loop back to line 47 to see if we've reached the final level.

You'll also see that on line 68 we're testing two conditions: the level will play if level_over isn't True and if the user hasn't pressed Escape. The event-handling code is unchanged, but we've simplified the code for adding new fruits to the screen: we're now doing this every time ticktock reaches 120, which, for level 1, will be 4 seconds (30 frames per second into 120).

On lines 95 and 96 we load a more interesting background, as an 8-bit PNG. The code then remains unchanged until line 101 when we add a new parameter to the update_position function of the Fruit class. We'll come to this when we look at the changes to that class.

Lines 104 to 110 have been enhanced to add extra player information. And on line 114 we call a new function of the game object to increment the level if ten raspberries have reached the bottom of the screen. We set level_over to True so that the level exits and Python loops back to line 47.

The only change to the last few lines (which we haven't reproduced here) is to add a summary to the final screen showing the player's overall score.

Game.py

```python
1    import pickle
2    class Game():
3        def __init__(self):
4            self._score=0
5            self._raspberries_saved=0
6            self._level=1
7
8        def update_score(self,amount):
9            self._score+=amount*self._level
10
11        def get_score(self):
12            return self._score
13
14        def update_raspberries_saved(self):
15            self._raspberries_saved+=1
16
17        def get_raspberries_saved(self):
18            return self._raspberries_saved
19
20        def update_level(self,amount):
21            self._level+=amount
22
23        def get_level(self):
24            return self._level
25
26        def save_game(self):
27            save_data={'score':self._score,'level':self._level}
28            save_file=open("savedata.dat","wb")
29            pickle.dump(save_data,save_file)
30
31        def load_game(self):
32            progress_file=open("savedata.dat","rb")
33            progress_data=pickle.load(progress_file)
34            self._score=progress_data['score']
35            self._level=progress_data['level']
```

The main change to game.py is to add the code for saving and loading the player's progress. So, on line 1 we import the pickle module. We've also added functions to update the score – on line 9 we multiply the amount the score changes by the level number, so the further through the game you get the bigger the rewards for hitting the right fruit (and the deductions for shooting a raspberry!). We also add functions to update and get the level numbers.

The interesting stuff starts at line 26. The code here is very similar to the examples in the section on Python libraries. On line 27 we create a *dictionary* containing the data we want to save (just score and level numbers for this game, but we could include the player's name for example). We open a file to save the data (if it doesn't exist, Python creates the file) and then dump it to save.

The `load_game` function is almost exactly the reverse. If the user had reached level 3 with a score of 1,234 when they pressed Escape, on restarting the game, `pickle` would load that data and `game._level` would now be 3. `game._score` would be 1,234, exactly as if they had never exited.

Fruit.py

```
1    import pygame, random
2    class Fruit(pygame.sprite.Sprite):
3
4        def __init__(self,WINDOWWIDTH):
5            pygame.sprite.Sprite.__init__(self)
6            self._species=random.choice(["raspberry", ▶
     "strawberry","cherry","pear","banana"])
7            self.image=pygame.image.load("images/"+ ▶
     self._species+".png")
8            self.image=pygame.transform.rotate(self.image, ▶
     random.randint(-35,35))
9            self.rect=self.image.get_rect()
10           self.rect.y=0-self.rect.height
11           self.rect.x=(random.randint(self.rect.width/2, ▶
     (WINDOWWIDTH-self.rect.width)))
12
13       def update_position(self,level,WINDOWHEIGHT,game):
14           if self.rect.y<(WINDOWHEIGHT):
15               self.rect.y+=2+level
16           else:
17               if self._species=="raspberry":
18                   game.update_score(50)
19                   game.update_raspberries_saved()
20               else:
21                   game.update_score(-10)
22
23               self.kill()
24
```

```
25        def shot(self,game):
26            if self._species=="raspberry":
27                game.update_score(-50)
28            else:
29                game.update_score(10)
30
31            self.kill()
```

We've made only a couple of minor changes to fruit.py. Line 8 rotates new fruit images by a random value between -35 and 35 degrees, making their appearance a little more interesting. You could add code into update_position to have them gently swing as they fell if you wanted the full effect!

Otherwise, the only change is on line 13, where we replace the speed parameter with level and then, on line 15, use that to increase the speed as the player progresses through the game.

Turret.py

```
1    import pygame
2    class Turret(pygame.sprite.Sprite):
3        def __init__(self,WINDOWWIDTH,WINDOWHEIGHT):
4            pygame.sprite.Sprite.__init__(self)
5            self.image=pygame.image.load("images/turret.png")
6            self.rect = self.image.get_rect()
7            self.rect.x = (WINDOWWIDTH-self.rect.width)/2
8            self.rect.y =WINDOWHEIGHT-self.rect.height
9
10       def update_position(self,direction,WINDOWWIDTH,level):
11           if direction=="left" and self.rect.x>10:
12               self.rect.x-=10+level
13           elif direction=="right" and ▶
     self.rect.x<(WINDOWWIDTH-10):
14               self.rect.x+=10+level
15
16       def get_gun_position(self):
17           position={}
18           position["x"]=self.rect.x+(self.rect.width/2)
19           position["y"]=self.rect.y-(self.rect.height/2)
20           return position
```

The final change we've made is to add the level number to the amount the turret moves each cycle. This has the effect of speeding up as the levels get higher;

Pi-Splat

Welcome to Pi-Splat

Shoot fruits but let raspberries through. There are 5 waves of fruit to foil.

Instructions

Press **Enter** to start a new game or **Shift** to continue an existing game

Use the **Arrow** keys to move your gun left and right

Press **Space** to fire

Press **Escape** to exit at any point

Our game is complete, including its own splash screen

otherwise, as the gameplay accelerates, the player would struggle to get across the screen in time to shoot the fruit.

Run the game and you should find you can play multiple levels and get a final score. It may not be of commercial quality but it's a complete, working game, and strangely addictive!

Targeting the Raspberry Pi

If you've been using a PC to create your game for the Pi, the last step is to test it on real Raspberry Pi hardware to ensure it performs acceptably.

Pi Splat could certainly be enhanced – with animations and explosions, for example – but since it isn't currently possible to access the Pi's full graphics capabilities from Python reliably, you may have to keep your ambitions modest. Once support is added, you'll be able to include spectacular graphical effects with very little impact on performance.

Sharing your game

Once you've polished your masterpiece, you'll want to share it. Exactly how you go about that depends on your target audience.

Sharing with Raspberry Pi and Linux users

Every major Linux distribution, including Raspbian, comes with Python installed, and Raspbian also has Pygame as part of its default installation. If you share your game with users of other distributions, they may need to install Pygame.

Zip it up

To share a Python program with other Linux users, you can simply compress the files into an *archive* (on Windows, these are called ZIP files) and send it. To do this on the Raspberry Pi, right-click on the main folder containing your game and select Compress. Then choose a file name and type for the package. If you're sharing with other Linux users then you can leave the type as .tar.gz. (If you want to share your file with Windows users, you'll want to change it to .zip – in this case, there are other some steps you'll need to take too, which we'll discuss below.) When the recipient receives this archive, they'll be able to extract your files, load `main.py` into Geany (or their preferred Python environment) and launch the game.

Clearly it would be nicer if the player could simply double-click a file to run the game. We can achieve this by creating a script file that tells the computer how to launch and run it. Here's how to do this in Linux: start by navigating to the folder containing your `main.py` file, then right-click and select "Create New Document | Empty Document". Give it the name `start.sh`. Now, right-click and select "Open with Geany". Then, in Geany type the single line:

```
python main.py
```

…and save the file. This is the same line you would type in at the terminal to run a Python file. We now need to tell Linux that it should execute this command when the text file is double-clicked. To do this, open a terminal window and type the following:

```
cd Desktop/Pi_Splat
```

`cd` is the Linux command for "change directory" and it simply tells the terminal that we want to work in the folder containing the game. Replace `Desktop/Pi_Splat` with the location of your game if you've saved it somewhere different. Now, in the terminal type:

```
chmod +x start.sh
```

The `chmod` command changes the "mode" of the file; in this case, the `+x` makes it executable. So, for example, instead of launching a text editor, the operating system will run the command. To see this in action, double-click the "start.sh" icon and select Run.

Sharing with Windows users

Windows doesn't come with Python installed as standard, so you can't simply send a Windows user an archive of your game and expect them to be able to play it. An easy solution to this problem is a tool called Py2Exe, which can compile your game into a single executable file that a Windows user can run with a double-click. The process feels convoluted the first time, but needs doing only once – and the person you're sharing with doesn't need to do anything at all.

To begin, head over to `www.rpilab.net/links` and download Py2Exe. Next, we need to delve into the bowels of Windows to make sure Py2Exe can find Python. To do this in Windows 7 or 8, press the Windows key and type

"Edit Environment Variables" as a search term. Open the Settings dialogue that comes up, click the Environment Variables button, and then, in the System Variables list, find the entry "Path" and click the "Edit..." button. Now, assuming you've installed Python 2.7 to the default location, simply add the following entry to the text in this box (making sure the entry before it ends in a semi-colon):

```
c:/Python27;
```

Save these settings and then reboot the PC.

When Windows comes back up, go to www.pygame.org/wiki/Pygame2exe and copy and paste the text in the white box on that page into a Geany window.

Download Py2Exe from the Pygame website

This is a template specifically written for using Pygame with Py2Exe, so, to get it to work for our project, we need to change the following lines:

45. change filename to `main.py`

48. Change project name to `PiSplat`

54. change project version to `0.1`

57. change licence to `GNU General Public License` (*sic*)

65. change description to `A simple shoot-em-up`

71. change the `self.extra_datas` list to include `images` so that the game images, in a subfolder of that name, will be bundled into the resulting file.

When you've done all this, save the file as `compile.py`, then open a Windows command prompt and navigate to the folder containing your game using the **cd** command. So, for example, if you've been saving the program files into a folder on your desktop, you might type:

```
cd Desktop\pi_splat
```

Now, to compile your EXE file type:

```
python compile.py
```

At the end of the process, you'll find a new subfolder called `dist` that contains all the files you need to distribute for your game to run. Double-click the file with the EXE extension and your game should now run. To share the game, all you need to do is ZIP up and distribute the contents of the `dist` folder.

Chapter Five

Creating a polished game

Back in the mid-1990s, Russian programmer Eugene Alemzhin released a game called *Shariki* in which the player scored points by matching three or more circles of the same colour. These circles then disappeared and their places were filled by the circles from the rows above, with additional circles randomly dropping from the top of the board to fill the gaps. Sound familiar?

Shariki was the basis of many popular games including the hugely successful Bejeweled series by PopCap Games and current favourite Candy Crush Saga by King.com. Together, this genre has become known as *match-three games*.

In this chapter, we'll look at a Raspberry Pi version of this game called Fruit Pi. Although (in principle) match-three games are relatively simple, creating a commercial-quality game is a more involved task than Pi Splat, our simple shoot-'em-up. So, we're going to take a look behind the scenes at the game halfway through its development. That way, we can discuss the game's design phase, the programming techniques used so far and what remains to be done before it can be released. The code can be downloaded from `rpilab.net/code`.

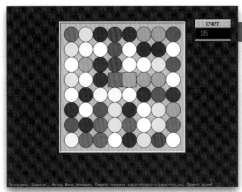

Shariki was the first "match-three game"

How the game works

As with Pi Splat, the first step is to look at the game from the user's point of view: what do they expect from a match-three game? Here are the basic rules, which are shared by most games of this type:

- The player sees objects arranged in a grid, usually 8x8.

- These objects are randomly drawn from a limited selection. In the case of an 8x8 grid; there are usually six. Too small a selection would lead to too many matches, while too large a selection would result in too few matches.

- The aim is to swap adjacent objects so that, in their new configuration, they form a pattern of three or more identical objects either vertically or horizontally. If no swap is possible, the objects return to their original place.

- The initial board for each level should contain no matches (this is why it is *pseudo* random rather than truly random).

- When a pattern is formed, the objects are then removed from the board and points are awarded.

- The objects directly above then drop into that space. Random fruits are added at the top of the grid to keep the whole board populated.

- If this change in configuration causes matches, the game processes them and awards points.

- The level is complete when a pre-determined score threshold is reached.

- Different versions of the game add extra features such as "power-ups" or rewards for matching the same object type more than once in succession.

This is a comparatively brief list of rules – it's not like learning chess. However, translating these simple requirements into a computer program is a different matter. Once again, we'll start by breaking the rules down into the familiar categories of input, logic and output to arrive at an initial set of tasks.

Input

The user needs a way to indicate which objects they wish to swap. In a computer-based game, this will usually mean by using a mouse. The final game will also need a way of reading in any saved progress data or stored game preferences.

Logic

The code must generate a pseudo-random set of objects *with no matches* for the initial board. When the player starts swapping objects, it must check for matches. When a match is made, the logic must identify which objects to delete as a result, move existing objects down the grid, and add new objects at the top to replace them. Finally, our game logic must keep track of game data, such as the player's current score and which level has been reached.

Output

From the player's perspective, the graphics, animations and sounds are what generate the experience of playing the game. So the game design, and the code we create to implement it, must include:

- Drawing attractive graphics

- Loading them into appropriate classes

- Animating them onto the screen

- Indicating which fruit has been selected during swapping

- Displaying the score and other game information

- Saving game progress and preference information to a file

- Playing in-game music and sounds

It's quite a list – and each of these tasks breaks down into many smaller programming jobs. Ultimately, we could be looking at hundreds or even thousands of lines of code. But don't be intimidated: as we mentioned earlier, many successful games have been developed by very small teams or individuals.

Fruit Pi

As with Pi Splat, we'll aim to get a single level running before going on to add multiple levels and the various other features that make for a complete, professional game. Aside from sourcing the fruit images for our game, we need to make several decisions, namely:

1. **The size of the playing area.** We've decided on a width of 1,024 pixels and a height of 768. This stretches the Pi's capabilities whilst still being large enough to make for a good visual experience.

2. **How we will indicate which fruit is selected.** The player needs a visual indicator. This might be that the fruit increases in size when clicked, for example. We've opted for a simple rectangle over the selected fruit.

3. **How we will animate fruit.** Many games make use of *metaphor*. We present the fruit as if they've been poured into the top of the computer screen from left to right, so we need to reflect this in the animation.

4. **How we will present user information.** Our 1,024 x 768 window leaves room for us to display information alongside the play area. We've opted to put the board on the right and the information on the left.

The game background is an 8-bit PNG file, and we've created a graphic for the board that's placed on top. We can refresh just this area when fruits move, saving processing power. We'll use sounds from `freesound.org` as before, but before implementing them we'll focus on getting the game mechanics and graphics working well on the Pi.

Programming approach
As with Pi Splat, each fruit will be based on a Fruit class, which will remember what type of fruit it is and where it's located on the screen. It will be capable of updating its own position and following rules about when to stop moving. We'll also once more organise our code into modules. The `main` module contains the game loop; most of the logic is contained in a `logic` module and most of the output code will go in a module called `display`.

Our fruit-themed match-three game, ingeniously named Fruit Pi

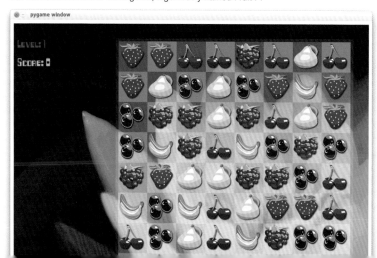

Under the microscope

Fruit Pi follows a structure that's typical of games, and in particular those games created in Python. The central module, `main.py`, contains the core of the game – the main loop – with most of the work of generating and displaying the visual objects and handling user interaction undertaken by an array of modules and classes summarised in this diagram:

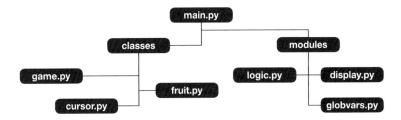

This structure provides good examples of the differences between modules and classes. You can see that each of the classes defines an object that has a clear, individual, identity. The `Fruit` and `Cursor` classes are graphical objects and the `Game` class is used to hold information about the game currently being played (including the score and level).

The modules, on the other hand, are simply blocks of code organised according to their purpose. The file `logic.py`, for example, doesn't define a sort of object: it's a set of functions that handles the program's decision making.

Similarly, the functions in `display.py` deal with the visual aspects of the game – including creating and handling the fruit objects. To use a juggling analogy, the class defines the balls and the module describes how the juggler throws them. We'll see this working in practice as we look at the code itself.

Modules, then, are mainly used to organise code into logical units, and they also make it easier to share code across projects. You could dump the entire contents of each module into the `main.py` file and it would still work, but it would be ungainly, impossible to reuse and hard to manage.

You'll have noticed that the module names are influenced by our input, logic and output approach (`display.py` representing the last of these). The only reason there isn't a discrete `input` module is because, for this game, the user input amounts to little more than clicking a pair of fruits, so it can be easily handled within the other modules.

The way you organise your code must make sense to you (and your team if you aren't working alone). And, above all else, whatever approach you use, it must be practical. If you ever feel you're being restricted by the structure you've created, then you've created the wrong structure!

So, from our thoughts on design and by using our input, logic, output approach we can very quickly generate a code structure for our game: we know from the start which objects we're likely to need and which modules to create. We may add or remove classes or modules as we develop, but by thinking in those terms we have a good starting point.

You'll notice one module that doesn't fit this rule: `globvars.py`. As its name suggests, this module contains all the `global` variables for the game. Now, mention the phrase `global variable` to programmers of a certain type and they'll throw up their hands in horror because, used inappropriately, they can cause problems.

However, it makes sense to use globals for variables that need to be accessed by all modules, especially where they are constants. We do this by defining them in a separate Python file and then importing it into all modules and classes. Here's the relevant code:

```
1    import pygame
2    ###TOP LEVEL VARIABLES
3    FPS = 30 # frames per second to update the screen
4    WINDOWWIDTH = 1024  # width of the program's window, in pixels
5    WINDOWHEIGHT = 768 # height in pixels
6    BOARDLEFT=300 #the position of the board, from the left
7    BOARDTOP=50 #the position of the board, from the top
8    CELLWIDTHHEIGHT=82 #the width of individual cells
9    CELLIMAGEWIDTH=68 # the width of the image files
10   BOARDWIDTH = 8 # how many columns in the board
11   BOARDHEIGHT = 8 # how many rows in the board
12   NUDGE=(CELLWIDTHHEIGHT-CELLIMAGEWIDTH)/2+4 #because the cell image is smaller than the
13   speed=30
14   WHITE=[255,255,255]; RED=[255,0,0]; GREEN=[0,255,0]; BLUE=[0,0,255]; BLACK=[0,0,0]
15
16   pygame.init()
17   displayFont=pygame.font.Font("256BYTES.TTF",28)
18
19
```

In the case of this game we're defining variables including the height and width of the game window, the position of the game board within that window, and the height and width of the cells within the board. We also define some common colours and a typeface.

The main loop

Let's look at the structure of a typical main loop for a game. Broadly speaking, this will be all that `main.py` contains, with all the other work being done by the modules and classes. We might characterise the structure of operations as:

```
#Import modules and classes
#Define variables
#Draw the background
#Game Loop
    #Level Loop
```

So, when the player first launches the game and the background has been drawn, they enter the game loop. Unless they've continued a saved game, they'll be at level 1, so the player enters the level loop that handles everything that happens within the level – fruit dropping into view, swapping, deleting and so on.

Once the level is completed, the player is sent back to the game loop (as the level loop is inside it). This checks to see whether the player was playing the final level and, if not, starts a new iteration of the level loop. This continues until the levels run out or the player exits the game. Let's take a look at how this works in practice.

Imports

We start by importing the various Python libraries we want to use on line 1:

```
1   import pygame, random, time, math, sys, copy
2   from pygame.locals import *
3   from game import *
4   from fruit import *
5   from logic import *
6   from display import *
7   from globvars import *
8   from cursor import *
9
10  game=Game()
```

pygame is the only one of these libraries that isn't included in a standard Python install (although it is included on the Raspberry Pi). Lines 3 to 8 import our custom classes and modules. With these we use a slightly different syntax:

```
from [module/class name] import *
```

The from keyword is mainly used to allow us to import part of a module. For example, the following line would import only the randint function from the Random library:

```
from random import randint
```

This is a more resource-efficient way of doing things, because Python doesn't have to import any unnecessary code – but it means that if you subsequently want to use another function from the library, you'd have to go back and add it to the from line. By specifying an asterisk we import everything, exactly as if we'd used the import keyword. This may seem to defeat the object of using from; but by doing it in this way we can refer to the functions within the module by just using their function name, rather than having to also add the module name. So, if we use the from keyword with an asterisk as above, we can turn this line:

```
my_number=random.randint(0,5)
```

… into the simpler:

```
my_number=randint(0,5)
```

In other words, once you've imported a function using the `from` syntax, you can use it as if it were built into the language rather than imported. This saves typing and, in many cases, is just as clear as explicitly naming the module.

There's one caveat to this approach, though. If multiple functions in separate modules have identical names then this will cause an error, so it needs careful handling. One way to do this is to use only the `from` method of importing with your own classes. This means that `game=game.Game()` becomes `game=Game()`. The first one must indicate which file the class is contained in; the second doesn't have to because we've used `from`.

This is another reason why you must organise your modules logically. If your code is to be easy to understand, either by yourself or another programmer, you can either prefix all module functions with their name by using `import` or, if you use the shorter form, have a logical structure to the modules that makes it obvious which one a function belongs to. For example, you could reasonably expect to find a function called `animateFruits` in the `display` module; you wouldn't expect to see it in `logic.py`.

Let's look now at the heart of the game – the level loop. This loop runs many times per second and carries out the following instructions during each cycle:

1. If fruits are falling (both at the beginning and when fruit is removed) draw the animation before moving on.

2. If not:
   a. Check whether any keys have been pressed or whether the mouse button has been clicked.
   b. If a fruit has been clicked on then:
      i. If it's the first of a pair, draw the cursor.
      ii. If it's the second of a pair, check whether the two fruits are neighbours (if not, they can't possibly match).
      iii. If so, run the matching algorithm and:
         1. If they do match, swap the fruits, update the score, delete the fruits, regenerate the board in its new configuration and animate into place.
         2. If they don't match, move the fruits back.
      iv. If the two fruits were not neighbours, set the second fruit to be the new position for the cursor and await a second click.

3. If no animation is taking place, refresh the screen.

This level loop continues to run until a pre-determined score is reached for the level, at which point it exits back to the main game loop. Most of the lines within the level loop call functions from modules or classes that carry out the actual work. For example, consider this line:

```
animateFruits(board,DISPLAYSURFACE,fruit_sprite_group, ▶
BOARD_AREA,board_graphic)
```

This single statement calls a 34-line function in `display.py`. Using functions in this way makes it easy to reuse the function elsewhere in this program, and it helps keep the code clear and easy to understand. Without knowing any of the detail of how `animateFruits` works, another programmer could look over the main module and instantly understand what the line does. So, `main.py` is, in a sense, a road map showing the primary route the program takes, with each module serving as a street atlas providing the detail.

Loading fruits

Before each level begins, the game must create a valid board. To do this we must first decide how the board will be represented; that is, what sort of variable can we use to store it? Fundamentally, the board is simply a table with eight rows and eight columns, and once you're used to Python you'll immediately realise that the humble list is the ideal variable type to store this. We might create a list for the bottom row of the playing area that looks like this:

```
('strawberry','strawberry','pear','banana','pear','cherry', ▶
'raspberry','raspberry')
```

To deal with the fact that we have eight different rows to handle, we'll make use of the fact that a list can contain other lists. In other words, we'll store the play area as a list of eight lists, each of which represents a row. We can then access the value of, say, the second fruit on the bottom row via the statement below. Remember that all lists are zero-indexed!

```
Fruit=board[7][1]
```

In practice, we rarely need to do this: it's easier simply to pull the whole row out and then access it in the normal way.

Now we've decided how our board will be represented, we can write a function that will create a new valid grid of fruits. The game loop runs this command before each level:

```
loadFruits(board,fruit_sprite_group)
```

As you'd expect, this function is found in `display.py`: here's how the relevant code looks:

```
16  ⊟def loadFruits(board,fruit_sprite_group):
17      cell_number=1
18
19      if len(board)>0:del board[:] #clear the board if there are any fruit objects already there (ie this is level 2+)
20
21      ####### CREATE FRUIT OBJECTS AND LOAD THEM INTO THE LIST BOX
22
23      for row in range(8):#run once for each of the 8 rows
24          thisrow=[] #each row is a separate list
25          y=row*CELLWIDTHHEIGHT+BOARDTOP+NUDGE #set the vertical position for the whole of the row
26
27          for column in range(8):#run once for each of the 8 columns in each row
28              exclude_fruits=[] #list of fruits that musn't be picked because they'd make an immediate match
29
30              if column>1: #check that the two fruits to the left do not match each other (not a prob for the first 2 columns)
31                  if thisrow[column-2]._name==thisrow[column-1]._name: #if the two to the left are the same as this one
32                      exclude_fruits.append(thisrow[column-1]._name)
33
34              if row>1: #now check whether the previous two rows hold the same fruit in this column
35                  if board[row-2][column]._name==board[row-1][column]._name:
36                      exclude_fruits.append(board[row-1][column]._name)
37
38              fruit_name=logic.get_fruit(exclude_fruits) #now get a fruit from the valid choices
39
40              x=column*CELLWIDTHHEIGHT+BOARDLEFT+NUDGE #set the left position of each fruit
41
42              this_fruit=Fruit(fruit_name,x,y,row,column,speed,BOARDWIDTH,BOARDHEIGHT) #create a fruit object
43
44              thisrow.append(this_fruit) # add a reference to the fruit object to the list for this row
45          board.append(thisrow) #add the whole row to the board, as a separate sublist
```

The use of two `for..in` loops such as this is very common when you want to represent two-dimensional structures such as a table in code. Line 23 runs eight times, once for each row – during which line 27 runs eight times, once for each cell in the row.

Line 25 sets the vertical position of the row, using the global variables to do so. By doing it this way we could replace the existing board with one of a different size by simply changing the values of those global variables.

Remember that one of the rules for the initial board is that it mustn't contain any immediate matches, so the `if` statements at lines 30 and 34 check whether a pair of the same fruit already exists to the left of the current cell or immediately above it. If so, then we can't use that fruit for this cell. So, we make a list called `exclude_fruits`, specifying those fruits we mustn't choose this time. We then call the `get_fruit` function in the logic module, which will send back the name of a randomly generated valid fruit. Here's the relevant section of `logic.py`:

```
120  ⊟def get_fruit(exclude_list=[]): #however many fruits there are, send back one randomly
121      fruit_names=["banana","blueberry","cherry","pear","raspberry","strawberry"]
122
123      for rottenfruit in exclude_list: #if any of the fruits are invalid
124          if rottenfruit in fruit_names: fruit_names.remove(rottenfruit) #remove them from the list of choices
125
126      fruit_name=randint(0,len(fruit_names)-1) #pick a fruit from the list of valid choices
127      return fruit_names[fruit_name]
```

Take a look at the parameters for `get_fruit`. You'll see that we specify `exclude_list` as you'd expect, so that `display.py` can send a list of fruit names we mustn't choose. However, most of the time this list will be empty. By setting exclude_list=[] we're telling Python that if we aren't sent a list, we can assume that there are no fruits, and to therefore use an empty list in this function. This is a default setting – it can be very useful if you aren't sure which parameters will be passed to a function.

We then create a list with the complete set of fruit names and, in line 123, cycle through the list of excluded fruits, removing them from the list of fruit names in line 124. The if statement in line 124 is needed because if, say, there are two raspberries to the left *and* two above, then exclude_list would contain "raspberry" twice – and Python would throw an error if we tried to remove it when it had already been deleted.

Lines 126 and 127 pull a random fruit out of the remaining candidates and send them back.

Once we have that name, we can create a new Fruit object for this cell. We then add this fruit to the row and, once we have a whole row, we add it to the board.

```
this_fruit=Fruit(fruit_name,x,y,row,column,speed, ▶
BOARDWIDTH,BOARDHEIGHT)
```

This calls the initialisation routine in the Fruit class and sends it the information it needs in order to create a fruit object. In this case, this means it will load the correct graphic and set its final position on the board. It also sets a variable called _moving, which the code will use later to work out if the fruit is still animating or whether it's arrived in place.

The other functions contained in the Fruit class illustrate how self-aware it is. calculate_new_position works out where the fruit should be the next time it's drawn to the screen. It takes account of whether it's travelling down the screen (as it would be initially), across or up (in the case of a swap), and also works out when to change the _moving variable to False so that the game can then ignore it during animation. In traditional procedural programming, you'd need to write a complicated nested list to track each fruit from within the level loop; here we leave it to the object itself to do this.

The calculate_neighbours method records the fruits above, alongside and below this fruit (where applicable). This is used later by the level loop when determining whether fruits can be swapped.

change_image is used when we swap fruits – this is because we're actually changing their image rather than directly swapping objects. This is a much simpler approach because it means that each object can retain its *x* and *y* positions in the grid for the entire level, and simply needs to update its fruit graphic to reflect the state of play. This function handles all the changes necessary when a fruit changes.

Animating fruits

animate_fruits produces the effect of fruit being poured onto the screen from bottom to top, right to left

One particularly distinctive aspect of games such as Bejeweled and Candy Crush Saga is the way the objects – gems, sweets or, in our case, fruit – fall onto the screen. When designing a routine for this, the first step is to write a set of rules for displaying the objects. Our rules are simple enough: first, the fruit appears from the top and fills the board from the bottom upwards. Then, fruit fills from the right-hand side of the row.

In other words, when building an empty board, the bottom right-hand cell is the first to be filled with fruit, and the top-left-hand cell the last. The implication of this is that we have to build a routine that not only adds fruit from bottom to top but also from right to left.

Remember, at this point we have a list called **board** containing eight sub-lists representing the rows and each containing eight fruit objects, one per cell. Our job now is to animate them onto the screen rather than simply plonking them there in one go (even though that would be much simpler to program!). To make matters more difficult, the row should fill from right to left rather than the whole row appearing at once.

The `animateFruits` function is contained in `display.py`, as you'd expect, and is called from the level loop whenever the `re_paint` variable is set to `True`. This will be the case at the start of each level as the board fills up and each time fruit is removed by swapping.

Here's the line that calls it:

```
animateFruits(board,DISPLAYSURFACE,fruit_sprite_group, ▶
BOARD_AREA,board_graphic)
```

What do we send to `animateFruits`? The board (the list of fruits organised by row), the Pygame surface onto which we're going to draw, the sprite group into which all the fruits will be placed, a global containing a `rect` of the board area (that is, its x, y, height and width), and a reference to the graphic itself.

The structure of `animateFruits` is similar to that of `loadFruits` in that we're iterating over rows and columns. This time, however, we're altering the position of the fruit each cycle.

```
51 ◇⊟def animateFruits(board,DISPLAYSURFACE,fruit_sprite_group, BOARD_AREA,board_graphic):
52        #global speed
53        ##### SHOW THE ANIMATION OF THE FRUITS FALLING IN STAGGERED FASHION
54        clock=pygame.time.Clock() #create a game clock for limiting the frames per second
55
56
57        falling_fruits=[] #create a copy of the board nested list
58   ⊟    for fruit_row in range(8):
59              falling_fruits.append(list(board[fruit_row]))
60
61        current_row=0
62
63   ⊟    for fruit_row in reversed(falling_fruits): #the "reversed" keyword starts at the end of the list and works up
64
65            fruit_sprite_group.add(fruit_row) #add all the fruit objects from this row to the sprite group ready to be displayed
66            n=0
67   ⊟        for fruit in reversed(fruit_row): ##stagger initial positions
68                fruit._speed=speed
69                fruit._current_y+=n #add n to the starting position of the fruit
70                n-=speed #makes n smaller (negative numbers) so the starting position goes up the screen off the page
71
72   ⊟        while len(fruit_row)>0: #while there are any fruits still in fruit_row (ie still in motion)
73
74   ⊟            for fruit in fruit_row: #for each fruit in the row
75                    fruit.move_me() #move it
76   ⊟                if fruit._moving==False: # if it's reached the bottom
77                        fruit_row.remove(fruit) #remove it from fruit_row
78
79                shrinking_board_area=(BOARD_AREA[0],BOARD_AREA[1],BOARD_AREA[2],BOARD_AREA[3]-(CELLWIDTHHEIGHT*(current_row-1)))
80
81                DISPLAYSURFACE.blit(board_graphic,shrinking_board_area) #only blit the bit of the board over which the fruits are falling
82
83                fruit_sprite_group.draw(DISPLAYSURFACE) # draw the sprites in their new positions to the surface
84                pygame.display.update(shrinking_board_area) # update only the animated part of the display
85                clock.tick(60)# Limit to 60 fps
86            current_row+=1
```

The above code shows the relevant part of **display.py**. We begin by making a copy of the board **list** – we'll see why later. In line 63 we begin the row by row loop; the **reversed** keyword specifies to start at the end of the list (the bottom row) and work upwards. On line 65, we add the entire row to the sprite group; then we work through each fruit (again using **reversed**; this time to work from right to left) progressively raising the vertical position as we go. This gives a staggered line with the left-hand fruit further off-screen than the right.

We then run each fruit in the row's **move_me** function, which launches the **calculate_new_position** function we covered earlier. We check whether the fruit's **_moving** property is **False** – indicating that it's arrived at its final position – and if so, we remove the reference to that row from **fruit_row**. Thus, we use fewer resources as each fruit stops moving, and we can use the **len** function in line 72 to check when the row has completed. If we'd been using the actual **board** variable, it would end up containing no fruits. This is why we copied it.

Line 79 calculates the minimum area the fruit will pass over as it falls. As the rows build up from the bottom, we don't need to redraw the settled rows every cycle, so this area becomes smaller and smaller. We feed this calculation into line 81's **blit** operation, which draws the board. We draw the fruit sprite group in one go but only update the shrinking board area. We could redraw the whole board each cycle, but this more efficient approach helps the Pi to keep up.

Once the board has been drawn, the program waits for the user to click on a fruit. Just as with key presses, Pygame can *listen* for mouse events, such as **MOUSEBUTTONDOWN**. Working out which fruit the mouse pointer was over when the button was clicked is handled in the **logic.py** function **which_fruit**:

```
112  def which_fruit(board,position): #work out which fruit is under the pointer when the mouse button is pressed
113      for fruit_row in board:
114          for fruit in fruit_row:
115              if fruit._rect.collidepoint(position):
116                  return fruit
```

This code takes advantage of a Pygame function called collidepoint, which receives as a parameter the event.pos returned by MOUSEBUTTONDOWN (this is actually two numbers, namely the *x* and *y* positions). Our loop simply iterates through each fruit in turn, checking whether collidepoint is True for that fruit. When it is, we know we're dealing with the fruit that's located under the mouse pointer, so we return this object.

```
56      if clicked_fruit: #if the mouse has been clicked over a fruit
57          if pair_of_fruits['source']==None:
58              pair_of_fruits['source']=clicked_fruit
59              decoration_sprite_group.add(cursor)
60              cursor.moveMe(clicked_fruit._rect)
61          else:
62              result=check_for_neighbour(pair_of_fruits['source'],clicked_fruit)
63              is_it_a_neighbour=result[0]
64              direction=result[1]
65              if is_it_a_neighbour:
66                  pair_of_fruits['dest']=clicked_fruit
67                  board=swap_fruits(pair_of_fruits,direction,board)
68                  result=handle_matches(board,pair_of_fruits)
69                  if result[0]==True: #if there were matches
70                      pair_of_fruits['source']=None
71                      game.update_score(result[1])
72                      re_paint=True
73                  else:
74                      if direction=="down":
75                          direction="up"
76                      elif direction=="up":
77                          direction="down"
78                      elif direction=="left":
79                          direction="right"
80                      else:
81                          direction="left"
82                      swap_fruits(pair_of_fruits,direction,board)

84                      re_paint=True
85              else:
86                  pair_of_fruits['source']=clicked_fruit
87                  decoration_sprite_group.add(cursor)
88                  cursor.moveMe(clicked_fruit._rect)
```

Back in main.py, we now check whether this was the first fruit to be clicked in a pair by establishing whether pair_of_fruits['source'] already contains a fruit. If it doesn't, we assume this is the first click, move the cursor over this fruit and wait for the player to click again.

Otherwise, the else at line 61 is triggered and we check whether the second fruit is a neighbour of the first. If it isn't, we consider this a "new" first click, since we assume that the player has found a match elsewhere. If the second fruit *is* a neighbour of the first then we must check whether there is a match and, if so, increment the score and update the screen. If not, we swap the fruits back to their original positions and go back to square one.

Finishing the game

So far, we've seen how the code builds a playing board, animates the pieces into place and handles the player's attempt at matching fruit. The next thing we need is some code to check that two selected fruits really are a valid match. The first step here is to check whether the selected fruits are neighbours. Here's the code from logic.py that handles this:

```
31  def check_for_neighbour(first_fruit,second_fruit):
32      if second_fruit._row==first_fruit._row and second_fruit._column==first_fruit._neighbours['left']:
33          return (True,'left')
34      elif second_fruit._row==first_fruit._row and second_fruit._column==first_fruit._neighbours['right']:
35          return (True,'right')
36      elif second_fruit._row==first_fruit._neighbours['up'] and second_fruit._column==first_fruit._column:
37          return (True,'up')
38      elif second_fruit._row==first_fruit._neighbours['down'] and second_fruit._column==first_fruit._column:
39          return (True,'down')
40      else:
41          return (False,None)
```

This code is pretty simple: remember that when we created each fruit object, we ran a function that established its immediate neighbours. Take a look at line 32 and consider how this would translate into plain English: "*If both fruits are on the same row* **and** *the second fruit's column number is the same as the first fruit's neighbour on the left, then they must be neighbours.*"

We then check the same on the right; then, in lines 36 and 38, we work out whether they are neighbours above or below. If any of these tests returns a True result, we immediately return this, along with the direction. If none of them returns True, we return False because we've established that the selected fruits can't be neighbours.

Assuming they are neighbours, our next task is to work out whether, by swapping the fruits into the place the player intends, a vertical or horizontal line of at least three fruits would be formed:

```
4   def check_for_matches(board,pair_of_fruits):
5       copy_board=copy.deepcopy(board) #we make a copy so that we can work on it without affecting the original
6
7       #first check for row matches
8       any_matches=False #use this to track if there were any matches at all
9       row=0
10      for fruit_row in copy_board:
11          col=0
12          for fruit in fruit_row:
13              if col<6: #we only need to check the first 6 fruits in the row
14                  if fruit_row[col+1]._name==fruit_row[col+2]._name==fruit._name:
15                      #are the two fruits to the right the same as this one?
16                      any_matches=True
17                      fruit._delete=True; fruit_row[col+1]._delete=True; fruit_row[col+2]._delete=True
18              if row<6: #again, we only need to check the first 6 fruits in a column
19                  if copy_board[row+1][col]._name==copy_board[row+2][col]._name==fruit._name:
20                      #are the two fruits below the same as this one?
21                      any_matches=True
22                      fruit._delete=True;copy_board[row+1][col]._delete=True;copy_board[row+2][col]._delete=True
23              col+=1
24          row+=1
25
26      return_parameters=[any_matches]
27
28      if any_matches==True:
29          return_parameters.append(copy_board)
30
31      return return_parameters
```

The actual business of finding matches is pretty straightforward. We begin by making a copy of the board, so we can work on it without changing the original. We then use our familiar double `for..in` structure to go through each row and column in turn. Note that at line 13 we only need to check the first six fruits in a row: this is because any pattern that begins in the seventh would be too short to be valid (the same applies to columns). For each fruit, we check to see whether the two fruits to its right are the same as it. If so, we set the `_delete` property to `True` for all three fruits. This has no immediate effect – it simply marks the fruit for deletion later.

We repeat this for the columns from line 18, and send back both the `any_matches` variable (`True` or `False`) and, if `True`, the updated copy of the board. This contains copies of all the fruit objects, with those that are part of a matching pattern having their `_delete` property set to `True`.

```
58  def delete_matches(copy_board,board):
59      #now assemble a list of all the fruits that are to be deleted
60      delete_fruits=[]
61      extra_fruits_needed=[0,0,0,0,0,0,0,0]
62      last_affected_row=[0,0,0,0,0,0,0,0]
63
64      row=0
65      for fruit_row in copy_board:
66          column=0
67          for fruit in fruit_row:
68
69              if fruit._delete==True:
70                  extra_fruits_needed[column]+=1
71                  last_affected_row[column]=row
72                  delete_fruits.append(fruit)
73              column+=1
74          row+=1
75
76      #generate the new board
77      row=0
78      col=0
79      for number_of_new_fruits in extra_fruits_needed:
80          if number_of_new_fruits>0:
81              lastrow=last_affected_row[col]
82              for thisrow in range(lastrow,number_of_new_fruits-1,-1):
83                  board[thisrow][col]._current_y=board[thisrow-number_of_new_fruits][col]._y
84                  board[thisrow][col].change_image(board[thisrow-number_of_new_fruits][col]._name,\
85  board[thisrow-number_of_new_fruits][col]._x,board[thisrow][col]._current_y)
86                  board[thisrow][col]._moving=True
87                  board[thisrow][col]._direction="down"
88
89                  y=-80
90              for thisrow in range(0,number_of_new_fruits):
91                  board[thisrow][col]._current_y=y
92                  board[thisrow][col].change_image(get_fruit(),board[thisrow][col]._x,board[thisrow][col]._current_y)
93                  board[thisrow][col]._moving=True
94                  board[thisrow][col]._direction="down"
95                  y-=60
96          col+=1
97
98      number_of_fruits_matches=len(delete_fruits)
99      return (number_of_fruits_matches,board)
```

The above code implements the `delete_matches` function – arguably the most important function in the entire program. This section of code removes fruits that have been found to be part of a matching set, and generates a new board with all the necessary changes made. It begins by creating two lists, both of eight elements (one for each column of the board).

Each element of the first list, `extra_fruits_needed`, represents the number of new fruits that need to be generated for that column. The second list contains the number of the last row that is affected by the changes, again by column. This enables us to simply ignore the rows that remain the same.

At this point, we need to think about how we're going to handle fruits disappearing and being added. From the player's perspective, when a gap appears, the fruit above drops to fill the gap. As we've mentioned, it's easiest to handle this by updating the objects in the relevant positions. So, if three raspberries disappear and the fruit above the gap is a cherry, we can simply change the bottom raspberry to a cherry. This starts at line 79, above. To provide the correct visual effect, however, we don't want the cherry to instantly jump down into place, but to fall from its old position to the new one. We achieve this by temporarily changing the y position of each affected fruit to the same as the fruit whose variety it's stolen. Then we animate it moving back to its original position.

Lines 90 to 94 deal with adding new fruits to the board – or, to be precise, assigning new fruit names as needed to fill the gaps where fruits have fallen down. We generate random names for the relevant slots, load in the graphics and set the new fruits above the board so they can be animated into place.

There's one final eventuality we must deal with: what if, after the player has matched a line of fruits, and the board has been updated, the resulting updated board itself contains new matches? This is easy to handle: once the fruits have animated back into position, we run the `check_for_matches` process again. The function doesn't care whether the board it's working on was created by a user swapping fruits, or is the result of being regenerated. Either way, it will check through and report any matches.

Because we've used modular code, we're able to reuse the `animate_fruits` and `check_for_matches` procedures to handle both the initial board and all subsequently generated boards with no additional work.

Fruits drop into place to fill the gap left by a match

Next steps

We now have a fully working single level. The next step is to implement multiple levels, along with a splash screen, instructions and a function to save progress. The graphics and animations will need a little extra polish and sound effects are more or less mandatory. However, adding additional pizzazz will impact performance. So it's important to thoroughly test the game on the Raspberry Pi, and optimise the basic version for this slow platform before adding anything else. If your game is intended only for more powerful computers you can omit this stage, but you're narrowing your audience. The best approach is to optimise as far as you can and add only a minimum of extra graphical overhead to the final game – that way, it should work well on all platforms.

Tips for programming games

1. **Get each part fully working before moving on.** For this game, the first step is to create the initial game board – so this was implemented before animation was considered. That was completed before the interactive features were added. This approach can mean updating code when you move to the next stage, but you're always building on a fully working foundation.

2. **Code, test, code, test...** Remember that coding is done in small steps: you write a line (or a short block) and you test it. It almost never works first time, so amend and test again. Only move on once it's working.

3. **Write it down!** Don't be afraid to pull out a pen and paper when you get stuck. It can be hard to visualise the effect of what you're doing sometimes, but by drawing a rough representation of what the player will see, you can work out the consequences of your code.

4. **Use the terminal.** If you're unsure of how a piece of code works, type it into the Python interpreter via the terminal and see what happens.

5. **Use the documentation.** Python has excellent official documentation at `python.org`, and on third-party sites such as `www.stackoverflow.com`. There's no need to struggle – the Python community is very helpful.

6. **Write the documentation.** Use the # symbol to document your code as you go. The code examples in this book don't include extensive documentation for reasons of space, but the online samples are heavily commented.

7. **Take a break.** If you find yourself struggling with a particular problem, take a break. It's amazing how often a solution to a seemingly intractable problem can pop into your head when you've rested.

8. **Enjoy yourself.** Give yourself a big pat on the back when you get each part of the game working. There is nothing quite like working hard on a piece of code, getting deeply into it, running it and seeing it work on-screen.

Chapter Six

Pi in the sky

The Raspberry Pi has a number of features that make it ideally suited to real-world projects. It's cheap, small and rugged, and needs only a modest power supply. In this section, we're going to discover how to turn a Pi into a climate-monitoring station that can take measurements of the temperature, air pressure and light levels outside – and save them in a form you can then analyse using a spreadsheet program such as Microsoft Excel.

We're also going to cover how to connect to Dropbox, so that our project can share its results across multiple devices. Finally, we're going to look at how to use a Raspberry Pi without a keyboard, monitor or mouse, so that you can use your Pi in a wide range of small-scale projects.

The project objectives

Every home, school or workplace has its own micro-climate, so by taking measurements, you are generating unique local data. You can record seasonal fluctuations, for example, or observe how climate readings relate to weather.

Here are five questions you might want to design experiments for:

1. Does higher air pressure correlate with higher temperatures and clear sky?

2. Can a trend in air pressure predict temperature and/or light levels? If so, how far ahead?

3. What is the range of temperatures experienced at your location this year? What is the average? How does that compare with the average at your local Met Office weather station and across the region/country? How does it compare with historical averages?

4. Is there a correlation between light level and temperature on any given day?

5. How does the length of the day vary during the year? Is the speed of lengthening/shortening consistent or does it change with the seasons?

The list of theories to test is almost endless, but we're going to design our experiment with these five in mind. We can always add extra sensors and code to enhance it later.

Equipment list

To answer the questions above, we need sensors to read temperature, air pressure and light levels, as well as somewhere to house them. You can hook sensors directly to the Raspberry Pi's GPIO pins (or via a breakout board), but we've opted for a system based on USB. This makes the hardware setup dead simple (no soldering required) and it also means you could use a laptop as the host computer if you don't have a Pi.

Specifically, we'll use the TinkerForge system (`www.tinkerforge.com`), which is made up of controllers ("bricks") that plug into the Pi's USB socket and sensors ("bricklets") that connect to the bricks. This tutorial has been written specifically for these components; find direct links at `rpilab.net/links`.

*   **Raspberry Pi and case** – any version (we used a Model A).

*   **Raspberry Pi power supply**

*   **4-port unpowered USB hub**

*   **Compatible USB wireless dongle** – see `http://elinux.org/RPi_VerifiedPeripherals#USB_Wi-Fi_Adapters` for a list of possible options. We used the TP-Link TL-WN723N in this project.

- **4GB SD card** – or larger with Raspbian and Geany.

- **Keyboard, mouse and monitor** – needed only for development; once we deploy the project, these can be disconnected.

- A **Master Brick, Temperature Bricklet, Ambient Light Bricklet, Barometer Bricklet** and optional **Humidity Bricklet**, all available from TinkerForge. We also recommend a 3m USB cable and mounting kit for the Master Brick, plus cables and mounting kits for each bricklet. The length of the bricklet connector cables will depend on your specific project; if in doubt, get the largest size. The mounting kits consist of four small pillars. Each sensor is fixed to the pillars with the included bolts, which can then be screwed into a mount of your choice.

- **Bird nesting box** – yes, really! We're going to use this to house our sensors and, optionally, depending on how you want to set it up, the Master Brick. Drill holes in the front and sides to allow air flow (if the holes are big enough for birds to fit through, use gauze or chicken-wire to prevent this) and paint it white to reflect heat. You also need to drill a hole in the back to feed cables through.

Choosing a location
The Raspberry Pi must be within range of a Wi-Fi router (unless you're able to connect directly to a wired network). The bird box containing your sensors must be outside in a position where it isn't exposed to direct sunlight at any time, as this would affect the temperature readings. It should be sited around 4ft off the ground and positioned so that there's reasonable air flow around it.

The Pi itself will need to be protected from the rain. One option is to attach the bird box to the outside of a house, school building or garden shed with the Pi inside. You can try housing the Raspberry Pi in a weatherproof box (don't put it in the bird box), but you'll need to think about how you're going to provide it with power.

This bird box hides a set of sensors linked to a Raspberry Pi inside the shed that has been monitoring the climate continuously since July 2012

Step 1: Getting started

Our development process will involve using the Raspberry Pi in the normal way, connected to monitor, keyboard and mouse. Once we have everything working, we'll move it to its final position and log into it remotely. Prepare your sensors by connecting the USB cable to the Master Brick and then connecting the sensors to the brick – do not plug these into the Pi yet (you can get further instructions from TinkerForge). Boot into the desktop.

Step 2: Install Brick software

We'll now set up the driver that allows the Raspberry Pi to communicate with the Brick – the Brick Daemon – and a utility called the Brick Viewer, which allows us to see the status and readings from the brick and sensors.

1. **Brick Daemon**

   Begin by starting LXTerminal and typing the following:

   ```
   sudo apt-get install python-twisted python-gudev libusb-1.0-0
   ```

This will install the relevant libraries. Then follow with these two lines to "get" the latest version of the Brick Daemon from the TinkerForge website and extract and install the driver:

```
wget http://download.tinkerforge.com/tools/brickd/linux/▶
brickd_linux_latest_armhf.deb
sudo dpkg -i brickd_linux_latest_armhf.deb
```

2. **Brick Viewer**

Once the Daemon is installed, return to LXTerminal and type the following:

```
cd /home/pi
sudo apt-get install python python-qt4 python-qt4-gl ▶
python-qwt5-qt4 python-opengl
wget http://download.tinkerforge.com/tools/brickv/linux/▶
brickv_linux_latest.deb
sudo dpkg -i brickv_linux_latest.deb
```

Shut down the Pi, plug the Master Brick into the computer's USB port and start it up again. You can then launch Brick Viewer (it's in the "Other" folder) and click the Connect button. After a couple of seconds, the Master Brick and Bricklets will appear. Click the tab for the temperature sensor and you'll see the reading it's reporting.

3. Installer Software

Before we go any further, we can make life easier for ourselves by installing Python's Setup Tools library. This will in turn make installing the additional Python tools we need to communicate with our various bricklets very simple. To install the library, go to `https://pypi.python.org/pypi/setuptools#files` download the appropriate version for your system. Once this has downloaded, type:

```
sudo sh setuptools-0.6c11-py2.7.egg
```

...into LXTerminal, replacing the `setuptools` version with the name of the file you've actually downloaded (the above line is for a Pi running Python 2.7). An `egg` file is the Python equivalent of a standard Linux package. It contains all the necessary files as well as setup information that ensures the package is properly installed into the operating system.

Once this process has completed, we'll have access to a new command, `easy_install`, which we can then use to set up additional Python tools with a single line.

Coding the basic app

You can download the code for this project from `www.rpilab.net/code`

We've now set up a working connection between our sensors and the Raspberry Pi. The next step is to make them programmable through Python. To do this, we need to install the language *bindings* – a code library that forms a bridge between the bricklets and our application.

Begin by going to `http://www.tinkerforge.com/doc/Downloads.html#bindings-and-examples` and downloading the Python bindings. Right-click the file once it's downloaded and extract the contents to `home/pi/tinkerforge`.

We now need to set up the library so that Python knows where to find it. Open a terminal and type the following:

```
cd tinkerforge
sudo easy_install tinkerforge.egg
```

The first line moves the terminal into the Tinkerforge folder and the second one uses `easy_install` to set up the libraries. We can now use `import tinkerforge` in any Python code we write.

Structure

We want our code to take periodic readings and then save them in a form we can use. If we intended our code to also process our measurements into charts and tables then we'd probably choose SQLite as the method for saving data, because it lets us retrieve the results using sophisticated database queries.

However, it's much simpler to use a spreadsheet application such as Microsoft Excel or Google Docs to analyse and graph data. So, at this stage at least, we're going to output our data in CSV (comma separated values) format, which can be read by all spreadsheet programs. It's a very simple format – effectively it's a text file, which, in our case will contain each set of measurements on its own row.

Since we want to make repeated measurements, our main structure will be a loop, exactly as in a game, except that the code will loop much more slowly – every 15 minutes in our case. You can, of course, pick a different interval.

Getting connected

Each Tinkerforge sensor has its own unique ID (UID), which allows you to have more than one of the same sensor type connected at once. For example, you might want to measure the temperature both inside a building and outside. The easiest way to find out the UID is to start up the Brick Viewer and click the tab representing each one; you'll see the identifier listed.

Once you have the IDs, create a new file in Geany called `main.py` and enter the import statements we need:

```
1   import pygame, csv
2
3   HOST="localhost"
4   PORT=4223
5
6   AMBIENT_UID="am9"
7   TEMP_UID="bPb"
8   BARO_UID="bMW"
9
10  from tinkerforge.ip_connection import IPConnection
11  from tinkerforge.bricklet_barometer import Barometer
12  from tinkerforge.bricklet_temperature import Temperature
13  from tinkerforge.bricklet_ambient_light import AmbientLight
```

Once again, we import Pygame to handle keyboard events, plus the CSV module to save our spreadsheet file. We then set up a number of variables including the UIDs for each of the sensors. Finally, we import four Tinkerforge libraries: the first is the code for connecting to the Master Brick and the remaining lines import libraries for each of the sensors we're using in this project.

Reading the sensors

For testing purposes, we'll write a loop that senses every two seconds (as waiting 15 minutes to see if our code is working is clearly daft). Here's the code:

```
15  def main():
16      ipcon=IPConnection()
17      barometer=Barometer(BARO_UID,ipcon)
18      temp_sensor=Temperature(TEMP_UID, ipcon)
19      light_sensor=AmbientLight(AMBIENT_UID,ipcon)
20
21      ipcon.connect(HOST,PORT) #connect to the master brick
22      pygame.init()
23      clock=pygame.time.Clock()
24
25      end_prog=False
26
27      while end_prog==False:
28          for event in pygame.event.get():
29              if event.type==pygame.KEYDOWN:
30                  if event.key==pygame.K_ESCAPE:
31                      end_prog=True
32
33          air_pressure=barometer.get_air_pressure()/1000
34          temperature=temp_sensor.get_temperature()/100.0
35          light_level=light_sensor.get_illuminance()/10.0
36
37          print('Air pressure: '+str(air_pressure)+' mbar')
38          print('Temperature: '+str(temperature)+'C')
39          print('Illuminance: '+str(light_level)+' Lux')
40
41          pygame.time.wait(2000)
```

It begins by creating variables based on the **IPConnection** object, and then one variable for each sensor. In line 21, we make the connection to the Master Brick. We then set up a loop that's very similar to those we used for our games: it keeps cycling until we press the Escape key.

Lines 33, 34 and 35 read the measurements from the sensors and convert them to the standard form: millibars for air pressure, degrees Celsius for temperature, and lux for light.

Finally, we print the values. Give it a go! You should see the current readings appear in the terminal every couple of seconds.

Saving to spreadsheet

For our project, we'll need to keep track of calendar dates and times of day – and these are complicated things for computers to handle. Thanks to the ancient Babylonians, our time measurement system is based largely on the number 60 (with 60 seconds in the minute and 60 minutes in the hour), which isn't entirely computer friendly. In addition, the Earth takes approximately 365.25 days to orbit the sun so we also need to account for leap years. A final complication is added by the fact that the same point in time will represent different times of day in different locations – and those times vary throughout the year. In the UK, we use Greenwich Mean Time (GMT) in the winter and British Summer Time (BST or GMT+1) in the summer.

What our project requires is a standard and accurate way of recording when measurements were made. For example, we might want to compare the time of sunrise throughout the year: if we stick to local time, that will seem to "spring forward" by an hour in March and "fall back" in October. The best plan is to use GMT (or its international equivalent UTC) throughout the year and add an extra column to our data that records how many hours to add or deduct from that to get the local time.

Fortunately, Python provides libraries to help with managing time. We need to add the following lines to the top of the code:

```
from datetime import datetime
import pytz
```

The second of these modules, pytz, adds time zone information to make the job of working out how many hours to add a doddle. Building on these, we can create a module called **get_formatted_time**, which returns the current time formatted the way we want it. We begin by defining a time zone using pytz's built-in definitions and calling it GMT. We then retrieve the current UTC

```
23   def get_formatted_time():
24      GMT=pytz.timezone('Europe/London')
25      utc_time=datetime.now()
26      the_time={}
27      gmt_time=GMT.localize(utc_time)
28      the_time['date']=gmt_time.strftime('%d/%m/%y')
29      the_time['time']=gmt_time.strftime('%H:%M:%S')
30      the_time['zone']=gmt_time.strftime('%z')
31      return the_time
```

time using the now() method of datetime before using localize to return the GMT equivalent:

Once this is done, in line 28 we create a date in the format "dd/mm/yy" using the string format conventions common across most programming languages. We do the same for the time in line 29 and then, in line 30, we store the current zone offset. In the summer, this will be a 1 because the UK time at that point will be one hour ahead of UTC. Finally, we return these values to the calling function in the form of a dictionary with date, time and zone entries.

```
33  def main():
34      ipcon=IPConnection()
35      barometer=Barometer(BARO_UID,ipcon)
36      temp_sensor=Temperature(TEMP_UID, ipcon)
37      light_sensor=AmbientLight(AMBIENT_UID,ipcon)
38
39      ipcon.connect(HOST,PORT) #connect to the master brick
40      pygame.init()
41      clock=pygame.time.Clock()
42
43      end_prog=False
44
45      while end_prog==False:
46          for event in pygame.event.get():
47              if event.type==pygame.KEYDOWN:
48                  if event.key==pygame.K_ESCAPE:
49                      end_prog=True
50
51          air_pressure=barometer.get_air_pressure()/1000
52          temperature=temp_sensor.get_temperature()/100.0
53          light_level=light_sensor.get_illuminance()/10.0
54
55
56          time_info=get_formatted_time()
57
58          this_row=(time_info['date'],time_info['time'],time_info['zone'],temperature,air_pressure,light_level)
59          save_csv(this_row)
60          pygame.time.wait(2000)
```

Back in the `main` loop, we've removed the temporary `print` statements that wrote temperature, pressure and illuminance values to the screen. We've replaced them with the code at line 56, which calls our new `get_formatted_time` function. Then, on line 58, we assemble a new list object that contains the information returned from this function. For example:

```
"27/02/2013,14:14:17,0,6.75,1027,594.3"
```

```
8   AMBIENT_UID="am9"
9   TEMP_UID="bPb"
10  BARO_UID="bMW"
11  OUTPUT_FILE="weather_data.csv"
12
13  from tinkerforge.ip_connection import IPConnection
14  from tinkerforge.bricklet_barometer import Barometer
15  from tinkerforge.bricklet_temperature import Temperature
16  from tinkerforge.bricklet_ambient_light import AmbientLight
17
18  def save_csv(line):
19      csv_file=open(OUTPUT_FILE,'a+')
20      writer=csv.writer(csv_file)
21      writer.writerow(line)
22      csv_file.close()
```

Now, all we to do is save this information to a CSV file. In line 11, we've created a new constant `OUTPUT_FILE` that holds the name we're giving to this file. Lines 18 to 21 are all we need to add the current measurement to that file. In line 19, we **open** the file (it will be created if it doesn't already exist). The parameter **a+** tells Python that we want to append this measurement to the end of the file.

We then create a new object based on the `csv` object and, on line 21, we use the `csv` library's `writerow` function to save the measurements to the CSV file as a single line. We then close the file.

If you run the completed code for this version of the program, you should notice the CSV file being created and lines being added every two seconds. End the program and open the CSV file in your spreadsheet program: you'll see that several rows have appeared.

Adding a summary

Our CSV file grows at quite a rate, and even once we've set the sampling period to its final value of 15 minutes (which we'll do by increasing the interval in `pygame.time.wait` to 900,000 milliseconds) – we'll still be generating a lot of data over time. For most purposes this is good. If we want to see if there's a correlation between light levels and temperature, for example, having plenty of data to choose from across any particular day is helpful.

However, if you wanted to examine the link between air pressure and average temperature over a month or more, it would be more convenient to have the data summarised and organised by date. Fortunately, the work involved in saving a second set of data is pretty minimal: all we need to do is total up the day's readings and then save them once per day.

We'll do this by creating a class called `Today`, which we can call from our `main` module at the appropriate time. This class has three variables (also called *properties*) to keep running totals of the temperature, air pressure and light levels. Every time measurements are made, we now add a function called `update` that tells `Today` to update its totals and check whether the day has finished:

```
32      def update(self,day,row):
33          newday=False
34
35          if day<>self._day:
36              self._day=day
37              daysummary=self.summarise(row[0])
38              newday=True
39
40          else:
41              self._temp.append(row[3])
42              self._lux.append(row[5])
43              self._pressure.append(row[4])
44              self.pickle_data()
45
46          if newday==True:
47              self.clear_values(day)
48              self._temp.append(row[3])
49              self._lux.append(row[5])
50              self._pressure.append(row[4])
51              return daysummary
52          else:
53              return newday
```

Working out whether the day has ended is pretty simple: all we do is pass the current day number to the function and check whether it equals the one stored by Today. If, for example, we took a reading at 11.50pm on 21 July, then today._ day would have a value of 21 and the value of day passed by the main loop would also be 21. Fifteen minutes later, however, the day value in the main loop would have increased to 22, as it would now be 22 July. When day was compared with today._day, the two would now be unequal and we'd set newday to True. You can see on line 37 that this triggers the summarise function and sends it the final set of measurements.

If it's not a new day, we add the current measurements to the lists and then save them using pickle (otherwise, if the program were stopped at any point during the day, all the previous measurements would be lost). Then, on line 47, today's variables are cleared ready for the new day to start from scratch and then the latest set of measurements is added to the new lists:

```
13      def summarise(self,date):
14          self.unpickle_data()
15          maxtemp=max(self._temp)
16          mintemp=min(self._temp)
17          avgtemp=int(sum(self._temp)/len(self._temp)*100)
18          avgtemp=avgtemp/100.00
19          maxpressure=max(self._pressure)
20          minpressure=min(self._pressure)
21          avgpressure=sum(self._pressure)//len(self._pressure)
22          maxlux=max(self._lux)
23          summary=(date,maxtemp,mintemp,avgtemp,maxpressure,minpressure,avgpressure,maxlux)
24          return summary
```

Once we've read the pickle data into the lists, we want our summary to include minimum and maximum temperatures for the day, along with the average temperature. We do the same with average pressure and also report the maximum light level – we don't report the minimum because that will always be zero (at night). We don't record an average for the same reason.

You can see that, because we've stored each set of measurements in a list, we can use Python's built-in functions to make finding the maximum and minimum very simple. Once the values have been calculated, we create a new list called summary and send it back. Now we simply need to insert three lines into our main loop to trigger the update:

```
98          newday=today.update(time_info['date'],this_row)
99
100     if newday<>False:
101          save_summary(newday)
```

Note that newday will either be False if we've simply updated the current day's running totals, or it will be a list if midnight has just passed. In this latter case, we then trigger a new function in the main module to save the summary:

```
30  def save_summary(thedata):
31      summary_file="climate_summary"+".csv"
32
33      if os.path.exists(summary_file)==False:
34          csv_file=open(summary_file,'w')
35          writer=csv.writer(csv_file)
36          writer.writerow(('Date','MaxTemp','MinTemp','AvgTemp',
                'MaxPressure','MinPressure','AvgPressure','Max Light'))
37          writer.writerow(thedata)
38      else:
39          csv_file=open(summary_file,'a+')
40          writer=csv.writer(csv_file)
41          writer.writerow(thedata)
```

Since there are more values to deal with, and it isn't necessarily obvious what each one represents, we're going to add a header row to the spreadsheet. So, on line 33, we use the os module's path.exists function to establish whether the CSV file has previously been created (in other words, whether this is the first time the program has been run).

If the file doesn't exist, we write a header row, followed by the summary data line. Note that in this case we use the 'w' parameter for opening the file: this is because we are *writing* a new file rather than *appending* to an existing one.

If the file does exist, the code in lines 39-41 saves the additional row in exactly the same way as with the 15-minute measurements.

Using third-party services

Python is powerful and easy to use – but what if the functionality you're after already exists in another service? For example, you might want to allow users of your latest game to be able to post their scores to Facebook (thus attracting potential new players). The social network doesn't give you direct access to its code, naturally, but it has created an Application Programming Interface (API) that allows your programs to talk to theirs. The API effectively specifies the rules for the "conversation" between your program and the service, and specifies which "topics" are allowed.

If you wanted to provide your users with a list of books on a specific topic, for example, you could do that by using the Google Books API – or direct them to their nearest bookshop with the Google Places API. You can embed Netflix's functionality into your app using its API, or save files into the cloud using Google Drive, Amazon S3 or the popular Dropbox service. Let's do that now.

Dropbox

Dropbox is a cloud storage service. Essentially it works by providing a special folder on the Dropbox server that's accessible only to the user. When you install the "client" software on your computer or mobile devices, the contents of that folder are copied onto it. Dropbox keeps all devices synchronised as files are added, edited and deleted – so, for example, if you create a new document on your PC and save it to your Dropbox folder, you could then access the same document on your iPad without taking any other action.

As well as client software and a web application for managing your content, Dropbox also offers an extensive API to allow you to access your files via a program. Given that there is no official Dropbox client for the Raspberry Pi, we have no choice but to make use of the API – but this is a convenient way to proceed anyway, since it gives us sophisticated access to Dropbox, enabling us to build complex and useful features into our code, without any need for user intervention.

Dropbox and Python work well together, not least because the Dropbox client is itself written in Python. As with most APIs, Dropbox includes its own library that makes connecting with its services possible, in much the same way as Tinkerforge's library makes connecting with its sensors possible.

Before you can do anything useful with Dropbox, you need to create an account (a free account is fine). You can then go to `https://www.dropbox.com/developers/apply?cont=/developers/apps` and, once you've agreed to the terms and conditions, click the "Create an app" button. This might seem a bit odd, but every program that wants to connect to Dropbox needs its own unique ID to identify it to the service.

Give your app a name and leave the "Access setting" value set to Folder. This means that any Dropbox user connecting to your climate-measuring app will see a new folder created in their Dropbox account called `apps` (if one doesn't already exist) and, within that, a subfolder with the same name as your app. In our case, we've chosen to call the app `RPi_Lab`.

On the "General information" page for your new app you'll see values for "App key" and "App secret" – you'll need both of these values for your Python code. Make sure to keep these private since they give the code full access. You're now set up on the Dropbox server.

The final step before we can start integrating your app with Dropbox is to download the Software Development Kit (SDK), which is analogous to the Tinkerforge bindings. To do this, head

Make a note of the App key and App secret – you'll need those for your code

over to `https://www.dropbox.com/developers/core/sdk` on your Pi and click the *Python* heading under Download SDK.

Once the SDK has been safely downloaded, right-click the file and select Xarchiver from the context menu. Extract the files to `home/pi/dropbox` and type the following into the terminal:

```
cd /dropbox/dropbox-python-sdk-1.5.1
```

Bear in mind that the folder name could be slightly different if the SDK's version number has been updated since publication; if the above command doesn't work, adjust your syntax accordingly. Finally, type this into the terminal:

```
sudo python setup.py install -f
```

This uses the `easy_install` library we added earlier to install the necessary Dropbox files. We'll now be able to access all the API functionality through a simple import statement.

Finishing the climate monitor

You won't be surprised to learn that we need authorisation from a Dropbox user before connecting to their account to upload the data. To handle Dropbox operations, we're going to create a new module called `upload.py` with two functions: `auth_dropbox` and `save_to_dropbox`.

```
 2  def auth_dropbox():
 3      from dropbox import client, rest, session
 4      import pickle,os
 5      APP_KEY = '                  '
 6      APP_SECRET = '                   '
 7      ACCESS_TYPE = 'app_folder'
 8      sess = session.DropboxSession(APP_KEY, APP_SECRET, ACCESS_TYPE)
 9
10      #has an access token been saved already?
11      if os.path.exists('config.dat')==False:
12          request_token = sess.obtain_request_token()
13          url = sess.build_authorize_url(request_token)
14
15          # Make the user sign in and authorize this token
16          print "", url
17          print "Please visit this website and press the 'Allow' button, then hit 'Enter' here."
18          raw_input()
19
20          # This will fail if the user didn't visit the above URL and hit 'Allow'
21          access_token = sess.obtain_access_token(request_token)
22          if access_token:
23              save_data={'access_token':access_token.key,'secret_token':access_token.secret}
24              save_file=open('config.dat','wb')
25              pickle.dump(save_data,save_file)
26              print "success"
```

Authorising Dropbox

Assuming you've installed the Dropbox SDK, you can now import the relevant parts using the `from` keyword as shown on line 3. We're also going to use the `pickle` and `os` standard libraries.

Dropbox works using *sessions*, which, for our purposes, you can think of as being one-off attempts to use the service. For each session you need to supply the application key, its Secret key and the access type (`app_folder` in almost every case). Dropbox uses these to establish that your application is registered with them and you, as the coder, are connecting legitimately (only you should know the Secret key).

Dropbox also needs to know which user's account you want to connect to and that you're authorised to do so. For this it requires an access token and secret token: these are different for each user and each session, and can only be generated when you're actually running the code. Since this isn't a publicly distributed app, some security restrictions apply: the Dropbox user must be either the person who registered the app with Dropbox (you) or one of the five additional accounts you can add on the "app details" page.

If you don't want the user to have to go through the rigmarole of authorising your app every time they run the program, you need to store these tokens to use again later. Not surprisingly, we'll be using `pickle` to do this.

The first step is to save the access information into properly named variables and create an object (`sess`) that's an *instance* of the Dropbox `session` class. We'll be using this to connect.

On line 11, we use `os.path.exists` to check whether `config.dat` exists – this being the name we've given the file in which we'll save the tokens. If it does exist then the program must have been run at least once before, and tokens must have been generated already and saved here. If so, we don't need to do anything further at this point.

If the file doesn't exist then we need to get the user's authorisation. Given that this is a program we'll be running ourselves, we can use a fairly basic approach to this; if you were creating a commercial app that connects to Dropbox accounts, you'd need to polish it up a bit.

The first step in obtaining authorisation is to create a request token that identifies us to the Dropbox server. Using this, we create a URL for the user to visit and authorise our access to their account. We add a `raw_input()` statement to halt execution until they've done this. Once they have, then the access token will be a property of the `sess` object and we can set a variable to its value.

This variable is actually a dictionary containing two tokens – the access token key and the access token secret – and we can then use `pickle` to save them to the `config.dat` file. Having done this, we can reuse these tokens in future sessions. To connect with a different Dropbox account, simply delete `config.dat`: the authorisation process will trigger again next time you run the program.

Saving to Dropbox

Now that we have our access credentials and are linked to a user's account, we're ready to save our data to their Dropbox folder on a regular basis. Here's the code that handles the actual writing of the file:

```
29  def save_to_dropbox(thefile):
30      # Include the Dropbox SDK libraries
31      from dropbox import client, rest, session
32      import pickle,os,sys
33
34      APP_KEY = '                    '
35      APP_SECRET = '                    '
36      ACCESS_TYPE = 'app_folder'
37      try:
38          sess = session.DropboxSession(APP_KEY, APP_SECRET, ACCESS_TYPE)
39          token_file=open('config.dat')
40          token_data=pickle.load(token_file)
41          access_token=token_data['access_token']
42          access_secret=token_data['secret_token']
43          sess.set_token(access_token,access_secret)
44          client = client.DropboxClient(sess)
45          f=open(thefile)
46          response=client.put_file('/'+thefile,f,True)
47          print response['client_mtime']
48      except IOError as e:
49          print "I/O error"
50      except:
51          print "Unexpected error:",sys.exc_info()[0]
```

It's important to bear in mind that Dropbox relies on a working network connection to upload the latest data. If a network error should occur to prevent Dropbox from connecting to the internet, Python's default response will be to exit the program with an error code, causing monitoring to stop. This is a potential stumbling block for such projects, because once the program is deployed we'll want the Raspberry Pi to run remotely, without a keyboard, monitor or mouse. This means that every time we want to reboot it, we'll have to connect to it over the network (if it's accessible) and restart the program. If we weren't able to do this until hours later, we'd lose a lot of measurements.

Fortunately, Python has a built-in mechanism for handling errors using the try statement – and its best friend except. When Python encounters the try statement, it knows that if any of the following code produces errors, it shouldn't abort the program, but should skip to the except statement later on to handle it.

In our case, we're instructing Python to attempt to upload the data (lines 38-47). If there's a problem with the network connect, an IOError will be generated and the first except block will run. In this case, it simply prints a message. Any other error prints some information to help us diagnose the problem. Crucially, in neither case does the program stop, so your data needn't be lost. As a rule of thumb, you should always use this technique when conditions you can't control directly (such as an internet connection's availability at any specific moment) would otherwise cause the program to crash.

Let's walk through the code in our **try** block. First, we create a new Dropbox session. We then open the **config.dat** file and use **pickle** to load in the access token and secret token we saved earlier. We then assign these to the **session** object, giving it all the information it needs to connect to the correct account.

We're now able to create an object based on Dropbox's core class – **DropboxClient** – which takes our **session** variable as its argument, and we have the Dropbox API at our command. In this scenario, all we want to do is upload a specific file to a particular folder, but you could build the complete functionality into your application if you wanted (for example, file browsing).

On line 45 we **open** the file and then pass it to the **put_file** function of the **client** object:

```
response=client.put_file('/'+thefile,f,True)
```

The first parameter tells Dropbox to upload the file; '**f**' is a reference to the file itself and the **True** switch ensures that Dropbox overwrites the file in the user's account. If we didn't use this (it's **False** by default) then Dropbox would create a new file each time.

The **response** variable contains various data about the file once it's been successfully uploaded. On line 47 we simply print it out so we can see, by looking at the interpreter output, that it's working.

The code is now almost complete: all we have to do now is add a few lines to **main.py** to trigger the Dropbox uploads:

```
68      pygame.init()
69
70      clock=pygame.time.Clock()
71      pygame.time.set_timer(USEREVENT+1,1800000) #upload every 30 minutes
72      upload.auth_dropbox()
73
74      end_prog=False
75
76      while end_prog==False:
77          for event in pygame.event.get():
78              if event.type==USEREVENT+1:
79                  upload.save_to_dropbox(OUTPUT_FILE)
80              if event.type==pygame.KEYDOWN:
81                  if event.key==pygame.K_ESCAPE:
82                      end_prog=True
```

Having imported the **upload** module into **main**, we add a call to the authorisation function in the main loop at line 72.

We've decided to upload the data every 30 minutes (in other words, after every second measurement) and this is achieved by line 71. This creates a new event that will be triggered every half an hour in line 78, at which point we run the **save_to_dropbox** function we just created.

Finally, we add a line to the `save_summary` function of `main` that causes the daily summary to be uploaded in one go after midnight. The end result is that every 15 minutes measurements are taken and saved to the SD card; every 30 minutes the latest version of this CSV file is uploaded to Dropbox; and then, at midnight, we calculate the daily averages, minimums and maximums, add them to the summary CSV file, save this locally and upload it.

Dialling into your Raspberry Pi

Our weather station is almost ready to deploy in its final position. The last thing to do is set up a remote connection to it so we can access the desktop from another computer – this means we don't have to have a monitor, keyboard or mouse connected to the Pi. Before we disconnect, however, we need to know its network IP address. Whilst this might change when you reconnect it, more often than not it will be assigned the same address, so this is a good place to start.

To find the current IP address type this in LXTerminal:

```
ip a
```

This will cause a lot of information to appear: we're only interested in the final line, beginning `inet`. Specifically, you need to write down the numbers that follow it. In most cases, the first three sets of numbers will be 192.168.1, so look for these and add the final one-, two- or three-digit number.

Finally, we need to install the software the Raspberry Pi will run to accept and manage connections. In LXTerminal, enter the following lines:

```
sudo apt-get update
sudo apt-get install tightvncserver
vncserver :1
```

You'll be prompted to create a password, which will be truncated to eight characters: this is the password you'll use when your computer connects to the Pi. You'll be asked whether you would like to add a "view only" password: in most cases, you won't need one.

We now need to set this server to run automatically when the Raspberry Pi is rebooted in its new location. To do this, launch the File Manager from the Raspbian desktop. Click View and then tick the `Show Hidden` option. You should now see a folder called `.config` in the `Pi` folder. Inside this folder, you should see an `autostart` directory (if it's not there click File | Create New | Folder). Right-click and select Create New | Blank File and name it `tightvnc.desktop`.

Now, right-click `tightvnc.desktop` and open it in Geany. You need to add the following text to the file (be careful to include the space before the colon on the fourth line):

```
[Desktop Entry]
Type=Application
Name=TightVNC
Exec=vncserver :1
StartupNotify=false
```

You should now be able to log in remotely. To test this in Windows, go to www.tightvnc.com/download.php and select the "Installer for Windows" entry appropriate for your setup. Download the installer, choose the "custom" option and deselect TightVNC Server (you only need the TightVNC Viewer). Mac and Linux users can use a built-in remote client or the Java version of TightVNC available from the downloads page.

Now launch the TightVNC Viewer and type the IP address of the Pi into the "Remote Host" box, following it with :1. Then click Connect. You'll be prompted for the password you chose and, once that's been entered, you should see a large window appear with a view of the Raspbian desktop. Congratulations, you've connected your computers together!

You can now shut down your Raspberry Pi, remove the keyboard, mouse and monitor, and install it in its final location, henceforth using TightVNC Viewer to control it remotely.

If TightVNC Viewer reports that it can't make the connection, this is possibly because the Pi's IP address has changed. In that case you can either guess by starting at 192.168.1.2 (or 192.168.0.2 if your network is set up that way) and moving upwards until you connect, or you can log into your router and examine the list of connected devices to find the IP address.

When you're ready to begin monitoring the climate, load your main.py file into Geany and run it. The first set of readings should appear quickly, confirming that the program is working.

What next?

You should now start receiving updates to your Dropbox folder every 30 minutes (assuming you're using the same update interval as in our example). The update will appear as a CSV file in your application folder. Make a copy and open it in your spreadsheet – you should see your initial readings listed. Remember to check the following morning for the summary CSV file. If that's there too, you know everything is working as intended.

TightVNC lets you access your Raspberry Pi remotely

Calibrate your unit

It's a good idea to check your readings against those of your local weather station. The Met Office's observations page at `www.metoffice.gov.uk/weather/uk/observations` will help you find the station nearest to you. If your value for current temperature differs from the "official" value by more than a degree then you should investigate whether your box is being overheated by direct sunlight (or cooled by the wind). You can check for this by waiting for a sunny day, then plot your temperature data as a graph. You should see a fairly smooth, bell-shaped curve as the temperature rises and falls. If you see big jumps in temperature then it might indicate that the box is warming up too much.

If you have this problem, try moving the box, shading it or covering it in aluminium foil to reflect the heat away. Otherwise, your readings won't be valid.

Next steps

Your weather station can be used for long-term studies, but it will start generating useful data very quickly, so it makes sense to decide on some short-term objectives too, to start drawing conclusions sooner rather than later.

Let's say that you're interested in the relationship between air pressure and temperature. Once you have a week's worth of data, you can plot graphs to see how they interrelate. Here's how to generate your chart in LibreOffice/OpenOffice Calc:

1. Make a copy of the CSV file and open it in LibreOffice.

2. Select the date column first, then hold down Ctrl and select the AvgTemp and AvgPressure columns – you should now have three selected columns.

3. Click Insert/Chart choosing the Points and Lines chart type. Click in the Smooth Lines checkbox and click Finish.

4. You'll notice an immediate problem in the chart: the temperature values vary over a much smaller range than the air pressure values. To fix this, right-click over the chart and choose Insert/Delete Axes. Now, under Secondary Axes click next to *Y axis* – this adds another vertical axis on the right-hand side.

5. Right-click over the temperature line (in blue, at the bottom) and select Format Data Series. Under "Align data series to", select Secondary Y axis. The temperature readings will now be plotted against a much smaller scale.

To draw any firm conclusions you might want to wait until you have a larger data set, so you can compare results in different seasons, for example. Ultimately, it's up to you what you do with your data – that's what spreadsheets are for, after all.

The end?

Congratulations! Having made it this far, you've acquired the majority of the skills you'll need for a career in programming. From now on it's a matter of broadening your knowledge in the areas that interest you, and then adding the secret ingredient: practise.

Python can be used for powering websites, creating mobile apps and programming embedded devices – in fact, there are very few aspects of programming that aren't open to Python developers. The Raspberry Pi is a perfect companion to the language, and perhaps you've already thought of how you can combine the two in all sorts of weird and wonderful ways.

My advice is to start by focusing on an achievable project that interests you, and then find out whether anyone in the marvellous Raspberry Pi community has created something similar. Build something personal to you that makes a real difference to your day-to-day life – perhaps a Pi-powered door-entry system, a heat-sensing robot, or a time-lapse photography setup. Or how about building on the games we've provided?

Always remember, being a good programmer isn't about memorising the names of commands and functions. It isn't necessarily about late nights slumped over a laptop tracking down a particularly naughty bug. It isn't the preserve of geniuses who dream code, and it certainly isn't a purely male preserve. Programming is for everyone. It's about doing something you love; it's the ultimate creative pursuit.

Go out there, make something fabulous – and don't forget to tell me all about it by emailing `kevin.partner@nlightn.net`.

WRITTEN BY • Kevin Partner • kevinpartner@nlightn.net
DESIGNED BY • Andrew Bunce • andrew_bunce@talk21.com
PRODUCTION BY • Priti Patel

ADVERTISING
ACCOUNT MANAGER • Katie Wood • 020 7907 6689

MANAGEMENT
GROUP MANAGING DIRECTOR • Ian Westwood
MANAGING DIRECTOR, TECHNOLOGY • John Garewal
EDITORIAL DIRECTOR, TECHNOLOGY • Tim Danton
MD OF ADVERTISING • Julian Lloyd-Evans
MAGBOOK PUBLISHER • Dharmesh Mistry
NEWSTRADE DIRECTOR • David Barker
CHIEF OPERATING OFFICER • Brett Reynolds
GROUP FINANCE DIRECTOR • Ian Leggett
CHIEF EXECUTIVE • James Tye
CHAIRMAN • Felix Dennis

ISBN
1-78106-138-6